THE BRIDGES
OF ROBERT ADAM
A Fanciful and Picturesque Tour

THE BRIDGES
OF ROBERT ADAM

A Fanciful and Picturesque Tour

BENJAMIN RILEY

Foreword by **SIMON HEFFER**

TRIGLYPH
BOOKS

To D & D

Contents

Benjamin Riley is quite justified to observe in his preface to this fine and much-needed work of architectural scholarship that "it is not too much to say that the bridge as an architectural topic has been neglected." And even for many of us interested in architecture and architectural history, Mr. Riley's detailing of the massive contribution made to this form by Robert Adam will be revelatory. With his brothers John and James, Adam led the classical revival in Britain in the second half of the eighteenth century, and did so across Great Britain at a time when attitudes to the cultural capabilities of the Scots (the Adams were from Fife and Robert was educated in Edinburgh) were prejudiced to say the least—as any reader of Dr. Johnson will be aware. Given this was the age of the Scottish Enlightenment, such bigotry was especially ignorant, and Adam's architecture, like that of his brothers, stands as a series of monuments to a golden age of learning and thought.

Mr. Riley has made an academic study of Robert Adam's bridges for the best possible reason: that nobody else, in the vast literature about this great architect, has. By doing so he not only opens up a new perspective on Adam's work, but also through his study proves his point that Adam built his bridges not in isolation, but to fit in with the context of the landscape in which they were situated and of any other buildings in the vicinity. The author explains that Adam did not just ensure the utility of his piece of architecture—and utility is rather more essential in a bridge than it might be in much other building—but also sought to create a thing of beauty and a work of art. And in one of the earliest examples in the book, Mr. Riley shows how the repeated use of a motif from the environs of Dumfries House—the obelisk—on the bridge in the park creates what he calls, drawing on A. T. Bolton, Adam's "total effect." But in his own attention to detail, the author is careful to remind us of the importance of not just Adam's choice of ornament, but also of his choice of materials, for helping to ensure that that "effect" was consonant. He also reminds us of the scarcity of bridges in the eighteenth century, and not least how that scarcity created in public places concentrated crossing-points of rivers, and with them centers of commerce and population.

He tells us how Adam learned to design and engineer bridges, and links this with his understanding and appreciation of such structures in the classical world, especially in Italy and France. The ubiquity of bridges built since Adam's lifetime, thanks to the coming of the railways and the

Foreword

development of extensive road networks in the age of internal-combustion engines, causes us to forget just what feats they were before the Industrial Revolution. One of the beauties of this book is the lavish way in which it is illustrated, reinforcing the message of the author's words both through contemporary photographs of the highest quality and reproductions of Adam's own drawings in all their detail and exquisite beauty—and of often unbuilt works by other visionary architects of the time, such as Soane. I recall as a child being captivated by Adam's bridge in the grounds of Audley End in Essex, near where I grew up: a design he made to complement a much older house. It shows how there can be great beauty in restraint, but we then see how Adam could gloriously represent power in his bridge at Alnwick Castle, which he supplied with battlements. Not only is this book an education, it is also a delight: echoing the very mixture of usefulness and aesthetics that its subject would so richly have praised.

SIMON HEFFER
Great Leighs
June 5, 2022

The first question I got, whenever I told someone about this book project was, "why bridges?" It's a fair point. They are certainly not the trendiest topic in architectural history, nor are they an evergreen, like studies of the country house. But it is not too much to say that the bridge, as an architectural topic, has been neglected. While specialist tomes on bridges exist, satisfying the appetites of confirmed pontophiles, their treatment within greater architectural history has been mostly tangential, regarded only as components of larger building projects. And while it is true that most of the bridges under discussion here were built as part of bigger schemes, that hardly means they lack value as independent objects. For a study of the bridges of Robert Adam (1728–92) reveals something greater about his work as a whole. No one doubts that studying Adam is a worthy pursuit—the continuing stream of new titles on various aspects of his work is clear testimony—but his bridges have gone more or less unremarked upon. And so this book represents a modest attempt to illuminate some aspects of Adam's bridge building, which will help to shed further light on his architectural practice as a whole. It is my contention that Adam's bridge work is the result of a keen attention to architectural context. While

Preface

other builders saw bridges as opportunities to create isolated monuments, Adam built bridges to fit within their settings and exploited the unique nature of the bridge to play off the surrounding architecture and landscape.

Adam built fewer than fifteen bridges, but nonetheless this book is not a comprehensive, cataloguing survey. Instead, it means to be a *tour d'horizon*, assessing underlying themes within Adam's bridge work and trying to relate them to his broader architecture. Where I succeed, it is on the foundation of the generations of Adam scholars who have come before me. Their exemplary works are attested to in the endnotes and bibliography, and they have my thanks for letting an amateur like me pursue a topic like this. Where I inevitably fail, I am entirely to blame. It is worth, before we proceed, making a small note on attributions. The Adams maintained a large office of draftsmen upon setting up in London following Robert's return from the Continent. As A. A. Tait has written, "transient draughtsmen kept alive the link between Italy and Italian drawing ... Grosvenor Street was a melting pot where the continual ebb and flow of such assistants kept architectural drawing and the Adam ideal of drawing in constant play."[1] But the presence of these transient draftsmen,

in addition to the fact that the Adam brothers themselves all drew, makes attributing drawings to the hands of a specific member of the office rather difficult.[2] As such, this study will treat drawings, unless otherwise identified, as being the work, in some capacity, of Robert Adam, who headed the Adam office and is universally recognized as the driving force behind the brothers' designs. When, in the early 1830s, the Adam family attempted to dispose of the drawings that now reside in Sir John Soane's Museum, David Laing, an Edinburgh collector representing the family in the sale, wrote to Soane. In his letter, he detailed the "immense mass" of drawings "comprising about Forty volumes in Atlas folio, chiefly half bound, at two different periods, filled with many hundred plans, elevations, etc. of public & private buildings—with drawings for Chimneys, Cielings [sic], Arabesque ornaments & other Architectural designs." These, he said, were all produced "either by Mr Adam [which is to say, Robert] or drawn under his direction."[3]

Now, without further delay, please join me on, to paraphrase the words of the architect himself, a "fanciful and picturesque" tour of the bridges of Robert Adam.

(1) **Montagu Bridge, Dalkeith Palace***
1792
Extant

(2) **Avenue Bridge, Dumfries House***
ca. 1754–59
Extant

(3) **Lion Bridge, Alnwick Castle***
1773
Extant

(4) **Ruined Arch and Viaduct, Culzean Castle***
1780
Extant

(5) **Bridge, Kirkdale House**
1788
Modified and disused

(6) **Bridge, Kedleston Hall**
1770–71
Extant

(7) **Bridge over the Cam
and Tea House Bridge, Audley End***
ca. 1763 and 1782–83 respectively
Extant

(8) **Hopping Bridge, Mistley**
ca. 1770–80s
Modified

(9) **Sham Bridge, Kenwood**
ca. 1767
Extant

(10) **Bridge, Osterley Park**
ca. 1768
Disused

(11) **Bridge, Syon House***
ca. 1763–65
Likely never built

(12) **Pulteney Bridge, Bath***
1770–74
Extant

* Bridge is featured and illustrated

The Bridges

Nearly forty years separate Robert Adam's first foray into bridge building, at Dumfries House in Ayrshire, and his last, at Dalkeith Palace in Midlothian. In his end was his beginning: he had started a Scottish architect and died one. In the intervening years his architectural practice took him across the United Kingdom, where he produced bridges as part of greater building programs, whether on estates, as at Audley End, or in public, as with the Pulteney Bridge in Bath. The stylistic malleability evinced by Adam's bridge designs, such as his moving from classical forms at Syon to castellated ones at Alnwick for a single client, is not evidence of a changeable mind. Rather it indicates a close attention to what he called the "adjacent scenes," whereby the bridge was meant to fit within its stylistic context.

CHAPTER I

Beginnings

In late November 1754, the budding architect Robert Adam was cutting quite a figure. "Once plain," he now possessed

> a most Frenchified head of hair, loaded with powder ... a complete suit cut of velvet of two colours ... set off by a white satin lining; white silk stockings and embroidered silk gushets ... Mariguin [maroquin leather] pumps with red heels

with "stone-buckles like diamonds" that shone "on his knees and shoes. A gold-handled sword, with white and gold handle knot, ornaments his side: Brussels lace, his breast and hands: a solitaire ribbon his neck." He was most proud of his "white beaver cap ... with gold lace round the edge of it and a gold button a-top."[4] All this was a long way from his native Scotland. On a grand tour accompanying the aristocrat Charles Hope, Adam made a curious choice, and it wasn't the velvet suit.

Rather, the curious choice was his itinerary through France on the way to Italy, the source of antique wisdom and the ultimate goal of most grand tourists. Adam "followed the usual winter sea-route to Italy—Paris, Lyon, down the Rhône valley to Marseilles, and then to Nice from where the feluccas plied along the coast to Genoa." But rather than visiting the usual halts of Orange and St. Remy, he instead stopped at the Pont du Gard.[5] At Nîmes Adam did see the Maison Carrée, the famed Roman temple, but he left no comment on it. By contrast, the Roman aqueduct at Chaponost was "most magnificent and stupendous ..." A special trip was made to the bridge at Pont-Saint-Esprit, under the mistaken belief that the medieval masonry structure was Roman in origin. Adam had been told it was "a most immense thing and the greatest curiosity."[6] Was Robert Adam a pontomaniac? That may be going too far, but what is certain is that he was continually engaged with bridges, which for him were not structures apart, but rather structures integral to their surroundings. But how exactly did Adam, a younger son of a Scottish architect before architects were celebrated, find himself on a grand tour, kitted out in the finest clothes, mixing with European aristocrats, and occasionally seeing the antiquities that were, after all, the ostensible reason for the trip? For that, we must return to Scotland.

OPPOSITE: Attributed to George Willison, *Robert Adam*, *ca.* 1770–74.

William Adam: The Progenitor

Any discussion of Robert Adam's life and architectural practice must first fly further back into the mists of the Scottish past, to the times of his father William: the first architect in the family, though not the first to be involved in the arts of building. In 1689, ten years after his father John's marriage to a daughter of the poor aristocrat Lord Cranstoun, William Adam was born near Kirkcaldy on the Fife coast north of Edinburgh.[7] John Adam in time joined the local "Incorporation of Hammermen," a guild of masons, probably earning enough to send William to the local grammar school, which was a fee-paying institution whose tuition included some Greek and Latin.[8] But any of William's formal schooling was mere prelude to his calling as a builder and later architect; as he put it, he was "bred a Mason and Served his time as Such."[9] There's some modesty in this claim; though he may have begun a mason, Adam quickly became Scotland's "universal architect," as John Clerk of Eldin, the chronicler of the Adam architectural dynasty, was to call him in his unpublished memoirs of Robert.[10] First, though, William engaged in various business schemes, often quite successfully. Sir John Clerk of Penicuik (Clerk of Eldin's father), who visited Adam in Kirkcaldy in 1728, listed "near to twenty general projects—Barley Mills, Timber Mills, Coal Works, Salt Pans, Marble Works, Highways, Farms, houses of his own a-building and houses belonging to others not a few."[11] So here was a man of industry, much of it owing to an association with William Robertson of Gladney, who became not just his business partner but his father-in-law. In 1714 the two men had jointly signed a contract to dig clay and manufacture brick tiles within the barony of Abbotshall in Kirkcaldy; two years later, Adam married Robertson's eighteen-year-old daughter, Mary.[12] By 1721

to his successful business activities he had added what we now call architecture, receiving a commission to build an addition at Hopetoun House, seat of the Earl of Hopetoun.[13] By 1724, Lord Polwarth, himself looking to remodel his estate, sought plans from Colen Campbell and James Gibbs, two of the leading London architects, in addition to plans from the Continent. But there was also another contender: William Adam, which shows how far the former mason had come in a decade. Polwarth wrote to his brother-in-law Sir James Hall of Dunglass,

> I would have you get Ld. Hopetoun's Architect
> who no doubt is the best in Scotland and have His
> advice about makeing it a good House & let him
> be pay'd for his advice, then see if what I propose is
> practicable, & about what expence Tho I should be
> glad to have a scheme from him & his advice first.[14]

While the scheme never came off, Polwarth's plaudits show the position of Adam among Scottish and even British architects. And Hopetoun and Polwarth were no rubes; both had been subscribers to the first two volumes of Campbell's *Vitruvius Britannicus* (1715, 1717), which promoted the taste for classical architecture within the British Isles.

Further aristocratic commissions followed, with Adam working on projects at Mavisbank (Sir John Clerk of Penicuik), Taymouth Castle (Earl of Breadalbane), and Redbraes Castle (Earl of Marchmont). Though of no famed stock himself, Adam was at ease with the great and good, as attested to by John Clerk of Eldin, who recorded how Adam was "attended with a graceful, independent and engaging address which was remarked to command reverence from his inferiors, respect from his equals & uncommon

Opposite: Hopetoun House, South Queensferry, Scotland. West front, enlarged by William Adam from 1720.

friendship and attachment from men of the highest rank."[15] Fulsome as the praise sounds, some truth must have been in it, for Adam continued to work on projects for Scotland's leading men through the rest of his life.

The year 1728 is a momentous one in our story, marking, as it does, the birth of Robert Adam. But it was also a major year for William Adam, who, in the span of those twelve months, was named Clerk and Storekeeper of the King's Works in Scotland, moved his family from Kirkcaldy to Edinburgh, and was admitted by the Edinburgh Town Council as a burgess and guild brother of the City.[16]

The Brothers

John Clerk of Eldin recalled the cultivated atmosphere in the Adam house in Edinburgh, saying that "the numerous family of Mr Adam ... formed around them a most attractive society & failed not to draw around them a set of men, whose learning, & genius have since done honor to the country which gave them birth." The list Clerk of Eldin sets out includes many of the worthies of the Scottish Enlightenment, including "Doctor Robertson the Historian ... Doctor Adam Smith Author of the Wealth of Nations ... Doctor Adam Fergusson Historian & Author of the progress of civil Society ... & many others whose superior taste & genius have been displayed in elegant & useful works which have rendered their names immortal."[17] Another friend of the family was David Hume, whose atheism offended Mary Adam but who was saved by his graces, which led Mary to believe that he was the "most innocent, agreeable, facetious man I ever met with."[18] It was in this intellectual atmosphere that the brothers Adam were brought up. As John Fleming memorably put it in his magisterial study of Robert Adam's early years,

While [William] Chambers was swabbing the deck of an East-Indiaman and [Robert] Mylne was hewing wood and stone in a mason's yard, the Adams were enjoying a liberal education in the humanities and were being forced to show their mettle in argument with some of the liveliest and keenest brains in an intellectual society hardly to be surpassed in any city of Europe.[19]

Education was important to the Adams, as it was to many living in Edinburgh during the eighteenth century. While John, the first son, born in 1721, received a practical education at Dalkeith Grammar School, being, in the words of his father "bred up in the knowledge of Carpenter work, as well as Mason's work & Architecture," Robert received the education of a gentleman.[20] At the Royal High School in Edinburgh, which Robert entered at the age of six, the main curriculum was Latin grammar, history, and literature, all suitable topics for future gentlemen. At the College in Edinburgh (later the University), Adam's set curriculum was Greek, metaphysics, logic, and natural philosophy, but his two known electives are revealing in light of his later interests: "New Philosophy," which is to say physics and mathematics, taught by Colin Maclaurin, who had trained under Newton; and anatomy with Dr. Alexander Monro, whose father had spawned a dynasty of medical teachers in the city.[21] The application of physics and mathematics to Robert's eventual architectural concerns is clear enough, while the anatomical studies would have been useful for his interests in drawing the human form, which remained even as his drawings became more focused on landscape and architecture. The 1745 Jacobite rebellion and an acute illness ended

OPPOSITE: Mary Adam, mother of the Adam brothers, was painted by Allan Ramsay in 1754, the year Robert began his grand tour.

Robert's studies, and by 1746 he had joined John in an apprenticeship to his father, William, who had in 1730 been made master mason to the Board of Ordnance.[22] But while Robert's formal education may have come to a close, life in his father's house constituted a continuing architectural education. William Adam's library included all the expected titles for one engaged in the practice of architecture, from four editions of Vitruvius to Leoni's editions of Palladio and Alberti, to three titles by Gibbs and William Kent's edition of Inigo Jones, as well as specialist titles in fortifications, gardens, and other architecture-adjacent fields.[23]

Such books would have been useful to the young Adam as he began work in his father's office, but no greater training could come than that which occurred as a result of the Adam family's hold on the master mason position at the Board of Ordnance. In 1748, William Adam had died, leaving a tidy inheritance and the estate at Blair Adam to John, while a smaller nearby estate at Dowhill, valued at £1,000, was left to Robert. The position at the Board of Ordnance, which had grown in importance with the Jacobite rising, passed to John, who brought Robert on as a partner in the enterprise posthaste.[24] Work on the construction of Fort George, in the Highlands near Inverness, was lucrative and surely instructive.[25] On his trips north, Adam can't have failed to notice the scores of bridges erected on Scottish roads by General George Wade, his father's supervisor in the Ordnance role and the man responsible for the creation of two hundred and fifty miles of new roads, all in the service of securing the Highlands.[26] These bridges, often single-arch designs in stark landscapes constructed of local materials, fitted their environments by necessity, perhaps leading Adam to consider how landscape and structure can play off each other.[27] Also enlightening was a 1749–50 trip to England, where Robert studied and drew various worthy buildings—

William Adam's library included all the expected titles for one engaged in the practice of architecture

including Wilton House, whose Palladian bridge he surely saw—and met up with the Adam family friend Paul Sandby, who gave him "hints" on landscape painting and doubtless furthered his sense of the picturesque.[28] Additional work followed at Hopetoun House, and all the while Robert was drawing, drawing, drawing.[29]

In August 1754, Robert Adam wrote to his mother from Dumfries House, in Cumnock, Ayrshire, "I thought to have wrote you by Tuesday's post from this place but really was so occupied with drinking and seeing nothing that it was not in my power to fulfil my intentions."[30] He had been busy in the usual Adam way, combining work with social activity, which was to become a leitmotif of the grand tour on which he would soon embark. The work was Dumfries House. This was the first major project he and his brother John had undertaken without their father, who had died six years earlier. It was not all parties for Robert, however much insouciance he might have suggested to his mother; the house's foundation stone had been laid a mere week before. Yet no amount of work could prevent Robert, in company with the assembled worthies (the architect was staying at the house as the guest of the Earl of Dumfries, his patron), from spending the idle hours "always merry and laughing."[31]

OPPOSITE: The principal façade of Dumfries House, Cumnock, Scotland, built starting in 1754.

Though Robert departed Dumfries House for Europe a few weeks later, documentary evidence suggests it is his young hand responsible for much of the house's form, both exterior and interior.[32] A pared-down design of three stories with its principal façade bearing a total of nine bays, with a pedimented central block and flanking pavilions, Dumfries House is a quiet, solid thing, far from the frippery Adam was to be accused of later in his career. The only ornament of note is an exceptionally intricate coat of arms within the pediment, which perhaps indicates a more elaborate scheme scuppered by cost concerns.[33] But though the house's design is shy, a motif in its front grounds, planted now with low hedge mazes, grabs attention. These are the obelisks, four in total (though originally only two), that give visual interest to an otherwise reticent façade. Now, follow the main avenue north from the house, to the foot of the Lugar Water, a river north of the house. Spy the obelisks on that bridge, four in total, each at one corner of the parapet. Here we see Adam's concept of what A. T. Bolton called "total effect," enumerated years later in his *Works in Architecture*.[34] A simple repeated motif gives the clue that the bridge is an essential part of the house, despite being separated by a half mile of road. And while the bridge no longer affords views of the house—the vista being now blocked by towering conifers— it did initially, setting a precedent for Adam's work on estate bridges, which tended to reveal the house from their span. Furthermore, the bridge served as the midway point between the house and the so-called "Temple," which was an elaborate gatehouse farther along the Avenue marking the new entrance to the house.[35] From point to point, Adam— and here it must be noted that teasing out which Adam, Robert or John, was responsible for a given detail is no easy feat—worked to ensure a unity of effect. Even in a project where ornament was kept as bare as possible,

ABOVE LEFT: The obelisks give visual interest to an otherwise reticent façade. OPPOSITE: Spy the obelisks on the bridge, four in total, each one at the corner of the parapet, providing an early example of Adam's concept of total effect.

repeated motifs are the primary way Adam attempted to deliver a sense of aesthetic harmony. And so it is no surprise that surviving photographs of the Temple gateway show it crowned with four obelisks—just like the bridge, which in turn echoes the two in front of the house.[36]

What the bridge lacks in ornament it makes up for in its handsome design. Let us begin on its northern approach, as a visitor to Dumfries House would have during its days as a private residence and before modern roadways changed the orientation.[37] The first thing one sees is a finial marking the edge of the wing wall, its circular shape echoing the splay of the wing wall itself, which draws the viewer towards the center of the span, from outside to in. A gentle rise, getting steeper as it goes, brings the visitor over the first of the three elliptical arches, small and situated still on the bank. Walk further up and you reach the center of the structure, marked by an obelisk on each side, with the obelisks sitting directly above the center of each pier. And of course this is not the first obelisk one would have seen, having entered the Avenue for which the bridge is named through the obelisk-topped Temple gateway. The Temple also sported finials similar to those on the bridge, enhancing the connection between the structures. Further visual appeal comes from the bridge's tripartite balustrade, which begins after the first of the obelisks, breaking up the parapet and providing a view of the Lugar Water. The bulging balusters recall the ball finials which they support, adding curves to an otherwise rather angular affair. And observe the way, even in this early work, Adam's idea of "movement"—that "rise and fall, the advance and recess, with other diversity of form, in the different parts of the building" —is present.[38] The low-slung splayed wing walls lead to a vertical obelisk, followed by a lower final; then we get another finial and a final piece of the balustrade before the last obelisk. The parapet begins to sweep down

LEFT: The tripartite balustrade breaks up the parapet and provides a view of the Lugar Water below. The parapet sweeps down in an early expression of Adam's taste for "movement."

again and the wing wall curves out on the other bank. The purpose of movement, "to add greatly to the picturesque of the composition," is fully in evidence. No mere conveyance, the bridge is a piece of architecture itself, and therefore needs to abide by the same rules Adam sets for all his other work. If the transition from the rising road to the flat center span is perhaps a little clunky, a bit rough, it must also be remembered that this bridge is an early effort, lacking the refinement that was to come from years engaged in bridge-building considerations both aesthetic and practical. The central arch does benefit from a molded arch ring, and the stone masonry is all incised to give texture to the surface of the spandrels and the voussoirs, but ultimately there is something unsatisfying about their elliptical shapes.

LEFT AND ABOVE: A molded arch ring and gorged stone masonry give texture to the bridge's façade.

The bridge is clearly related to another early example by the Adam brothers, Frew's Bridge at Inveraray (1756), illustrated in *Vitruvius Scoticus* and attributed to James Adam, especially in the flatness of the ellipse in the bridge's central arch.[39] Another bridge at Inveraray, illustrated on the same page in *Vitruvius Scoticus*, provided a model for a balustraded rise giving way to a picturesque view, Roger Morris's Garron Bridge. William Adam had in 1746 obtained the post of Intendant General at Inveraray to supervise Roger Morris's architecture. And though he evinced no great sympathy for the Gothic elements of the castle, he was keen on Morris's bridge, which was classically simple. And it was not just the steep rise that the Dumfries bridge borrowed, but the balustrade and ball-finial scheme. Where Morris has four finials topping the balustrade piers, Adam has chosen instead to replace the outer balustrade finials with obelisks, while also inserting finials at the end of each parapet, thereby linking the edges of the bridge to its center. The replacement of Morris's outer finials with obelisks, and the moving of those finials to each end of the bridge, achieves a wonderfully strategic harmony, linking each part of the bridge to another; simultaneously the bridge is related to the other major architectural parts of the Dumfries House estate, the house proper and the Temple gateway. The obelisks themselves have a family connection, recalling as they do the obelisks atop the piers of William Adam's famous bridge for General Wade at Aberfeldy.[40]

Was Robert Adam responsible for the design of the Avenue Bridge at Dumfries House? Does it matter? The bridge has traditionally been attributed to John, and this is understandable, given his superintending of the entire Dumfries House project.[41] John Adam even spelled out the cost for the bridge, specifying £430.16.2.[42] Perhaps John did design it; it's comfortable enough to assume that the bridge's plainness is the result

BRIDGE over the GARRAN

of John's somewhat more practical architectural mind, and the surviving original drawing from 1754 does appear to be in John's hand. But the elaborate scheme incorporating both obelisks and finials gives one pause in being too sure of the attribution. That the obelisks do not appear as part of the worked-up original drawing and instead are sketched on in pencil is one clue that perhaps the design was subject to Robert's typical exuberance at a later stage. Moreover, the balustrade in the original drawing is a wan thing, covering only a bare portion of the central arch, whereas the built balustrade covers the entirety of the central arch, going beyond its dimensions to reach the obelisk that sits above the pier. Such a balustrade brings to mind Robert Adam's work from years later at Audley End. While the precise attribution remains a mystery, we can be certain Robert was involved at some level in the bridge's design, for he kept abreast of the progress on the house even while on his grand tour.

The lessons he learned proved useful over a lifetime of bridge building. Perhaps just as useful were the social graces Robert honed while in Europe, which, combined with aristocratic contacts made on the Continent, provided him with a base of potential clients upon his return to Britain in 1758. His aggressive social strategy had worked. When he arrived in London he found himself, in the words of John Summerson, "besieged with clients."[43] Major commissions followed at Syon (the Duke of Northumberland), Kedleston (Baron Scarsdale), and Osterley (Sir Francis Child). Adam, owing to the patronage of his countryman Lord Bute, was made in 1761 "Architect of the King's Works."[44] Indeed, Lord Deskford predicted in an early 1761 letter to James Adam that Robert would soon initiate "a reign in Britain of Taste and Architecture."[45] All this success, combined with his winning a seat in Parliament in 1768, convinced Adam that he might finally fulfill his ambition for a great public building project, public buildings being "the most splendid monuments of a great and opulent people. The purpose for which they are intended admit of a magnificence in the design and require solidity in contraction."[46] This ambition was realized, with some success, at the Adelphi Terrace in London.[47] But such are concerns for another book. Let us instead focus on another element of Adam's immense corpus: his bridges.

ABOVE: Roger Morris's Bridge over the Garron, at Inveraray. From William Adam's *Vitruvius Scoticus*, published posthumously in 1810.

CHAPTER II

Bridges in Eighteenth-Century Britain

The bridge has always been regarded as a transitional structure—not purely a work of engineering, nor simply a work of architecture. Its functional requirements are more stringent than those of the average building: the bridge not only must stand up; it must stand up, support those who cross it, and effectively span the space over which it stands. As Samuel Johnson said, "the first excellence of a bridge is strength ... for a bridge that cannot stand, however beautiful, will boast its beauty but a little while."[48] Such elevated physical necessities limit what forms bridges can take. Yet because bridges are exempt from the constraints inherent in other types of buildings—which must provide suitable structures for people to inhabit continuously—they often present themselves as architectural statements: showpieces displaying the designer's skill, learning, or fashionability. Two strands emerge in eighteenth-century bridge building. Architects who saw bridges as worthy monuments to their learning and taste created "triumphal-type" bridges in major urban projects and related "Palladian" estate bridges: these bridges serve as scaffolding for applied architectural elements. Robert Adam was among those who took a different approach, seeking to locate bridges within an appropriate stylistic context, recognizing the bridge as part of a greater tableau, whether in cities or on estates.

While the first school saw bridges as little more than structures on which to hang ornament, the second apprehended the way bridges present opportunities that most buildings do not—specifically, opportunities for views. Bridges can serve as viewing platforms, allowing panoramic observation in a way that a house never can. They lay their structure bare: when we view a bridge from the ground, we view its arches and spandrels, the very elements that allow it to serve as an observing platform. Finally, since bridges provide for a crossing, whereby the view changes as one progresses over it, they can lead to other buildings, introduce them, and reference them, in ways that other types of structure cannot. Adam was aware of bridges' specific potentialities and his designs exploited these elements.

Despite the unique position occupied by bridges in the architectural space, they have been relatively little studied by architectural historians, treated often as engineering works devoid of much aesthetic interest. Robert Adam's work with bridges is similarly recondite. While Adam has received significant attention for other aspects of his architectural

Opposite: John Boydell, *A View of London Bridge taken near St. Olave's Stairs*, 1751. Clutter on bridges later gave way to clear vistas.

practice—building, interior decoration, picturesque drawing—his bridges have gone mostly unmentioned or have been summarily treated in larger catalogues of his work.[49] This study treats Adam's bridge projects synthetically, both as part of his own corpus, and within the context of bridge building in the later eighteenth century. Though Adam's bridges comprise but a small part of his immense body of work, his bridge work exceeds that of most of his contemporaries.[50] Moreover, his interest in bridges was not limited to commissioned projects. Over 100 bridge drawings survive in the Soane Museum's collection, most of them in Robert Adam's own hand.[51] Adam had an abiding interest in bridges and was continuously engaged with their design and execution throughout his long career. This book will consider the sources and results of Adam's fascination with bridges, concurrently situating Adam's work within the greater impulse for "improvement."

Before appraising Robert Adam's bridge work, it will be important to survey the state of bridge building in the era of his practice, roughly 1750 to 1791. Later eighteenth-century British bridges fall into one of two categories: public (military, civic, county) or private estate bridges. Each type was the product of a conscious drive for physical "improvement," which manifested itself disparately but included the building of bridges and roads in addition to the implementation of new agricultural methods, afforestation schemes, town planning, the remodeling of both public and private buildings, and much else.[52] Improvement, as a goal, was widespread in Georgian Britain, undertaken by civic bodies and fashionably pursued by aristocrats on their estates.[53]

Indicative of this, and especially relevant to later bridge building, is the process behind the commissioning and construction of Westminster Bridge (1738–50). Until Westminster Bridge's completion, the Thames was crossed in London only by the then-current iteration of London Bridge, now called "Old London Bridge," which had stood since the thirteenth century.[54] Built of stone, London Bridge was, by the 1730s,

Vüe du Pont de Westminster du Côté du Nord de Londres

Until Westminster Bridge's completion, the Thames was crossed in London only by the then-current iteration of London Bridge, now called "Old London Bridge"

OPPOSITE: Balthaazar F. Leizelt (active 1750–1800), after Charles
Labelye, *Vue du Pont de Westminister du Cote du Nord de Londres*.
ABOVE: Claude de Jongh, *View of London Bridge*, 1632.
London Bridge really was falling down.

in a feeble state: "narrow and dirty, its roadway contracted by houses and fouled by horses and cattle ... it was a major obstacle to the flow of the river and the movement of numerous river craft."[55] It was accepted that a new bridge would be necessary to reduce traffic around Westminster, and yet opposition to its construction was strident: the City characteristically resisted "public improvements outside their territory and in the slightest degree liable to injure their monopolies."[56] Joining the opposition were the ferrymen, who had enjoyed centuries of precedence in river trade. Adding to the suspicion of the project was the widespread conviction that England lacked engineers capable of designing and executing a bridge spanning 1,200 feet (the width of the river in the proposed building spot). The spirit of improvement prevailed, however, following the usual pattern for the period whereby the idea was adjudicated publicly, in the form of pamphlets, leading to the raising of a subscription fund for surveys of the river, the drafting of a Parliamentary Bill, and the provision of expert testimony for the Bill once in committee.[57] One of the pamphlets was written by an aged Nicholas Hawksmoor, who considered various questions of engineering in proposing a design; the title, which alludes to bridges "abroad," hints at the truth of the supposition that contemporary English models for complex masonry bridges could not be readily found.[58] That Hawksmoor, an architect, should be so involved in the bridge's creation, is suggestive of the nebulous distinction between architects and engineers in the period. As J. Mordaunt Crook has shown, the splitting of disciplines surrounding architecture was a product of the 1830s and later: "for architects and engineers, the eighteenth century recognized no viable distinction between them; and even as late as the 1840s the lines of demarcation were easily blurred."[59]

The design and construction of Westminster Bridge fell to a Huguenot, Charles Labelye.[60] His bridge took the form of thirteen semicircular arches,

LEFT: A bridge comes along bit by bit. Samuel Scott, *The Building of Westminster Bridge with an Imaginary View of Westminster Abbey, ca.* 1742.

faced in Portland stone, filled underneath with Purbeck stone, and with a balustraded parapet and projecting "turrets" rising from the cutwaters below, terminating in small ornamental domes. This was, above all, a feat of engineering in the sense that its structural facts were, in the words of John Summerson, "simply and gracefully expressed in the pattern of the masonry."[61] Westminster Bridge's unornamented design, with hardly a stone spared for decoration, emphasizes its sturdiness and durability. Any public doubts about the safety of such a long span could be allayed by the bridge's robust and rugged form. If the main public concern was the bridge's ability to stand up, then a rustic, relatively unadorned façade could suggest that the bridge builder's priorities were correctly aligned.

Westminster Bridge inaugurated an era of major masonry bridge building in Britain; Bernard Forest de Bélidor, the foremost writer on hydraulic engineering of the period, considered this new Thames crossing "the most magnificent monument of our times."[62] Bélidor's book served as a practical guide for would-be bridge builders. A copy of *Architecture Hydraulique*, likely bought while Adam was in Paris in 1754, was kept in the library at Blair Adam, the family home.[63]

There was an observable increase in plans for the improvement of London in the decades following Westminster Bridge's construction. This improving spirit manifested itself not only in tangible achievements— roads widened and paved, lighting installed, ditches like the Fleet filled in—but also in projects like those put forward in John Gwynn's *London and Westminster Improved* (1766), which suggested countless improvements, many of which were taken up in the decades following.[64] One for which Gwynn cannot receive credit is Blackfriars Bridge, which was commissioned by the City in 1756 and coincided with a restoration project on London Bridge.[65] In 1759 an advertisement was placed for designs, of which

Westminster Bridge inaugurated an era of major masonry bridge building in Britain

sixty-nine were submitted, a remarkable number given the difficulty in finding a single capable designer of Westminster Bridge just a few decades prior.[66] The list of entrants includes luminaries of the day: William Chambers, John Smeaton, Isaac Ware, John Gwynn, George Dance the Elder, and Robert Adam, just then returned from his travels on the Continent.[67] The commission went to Robert Mylne, also recently back from a period of study in Rome.[68]

The public debate that eventually resulted in Mylne's design winning the competition shows the exceptional position bridges occupied in contemporary London. No less a figure than Samuel Johnson agitated for a bridge with semicircular arches, arguing on both aesthetic and (erroneous) engineering terms. Mylne answered anonymously, in a pamphlet signed "Publicus," which set out the case for his elliptical-arch design and assuaged any lingering doubts the committee had.[69] That private individuals could engage in a serious, if not entirely learned, debate concerning bridge engineering shows how consuming the improvement impulse was in the eighteenth century.

Mylne's design of nine arches drew on the by-then-totemic Westminster Bridge while simultaneously engaging with newly fashionable ideas of bridge building. In the period since the construction of Westminster Bridge, British bridge design had been transformed by the return of a generation of would-be designers from Europe. Robert Adam seems to

OPPOSITE: Samuel Scott, *Arches of Westminster Bridge, ca.* 1750. The design inaugurated an era of major masonry bridge building in Britain. According to Bélidor, Westminster Bridge was "the most magnificent monument of our times."

have been especially intrigued by the engineering of the Roman world. Recall that while traveling the Continent he reserved his greatest praise for the aqueduct at Chaponost, finding it "so entire that I numbered a hundred arches all in a straight line which were most [magni]ficent and stupendous" and had made a special trip to the bridge at Pont-Saint-Esprit, under the mistaken belief that the medieval masonry structure was Roman in origin.[70] In Rome and the surrounding countryside, Adam and the other Blackfriars entrants had observed bridges, both antique and contemporary, and applied elements of these models to their own work, thereby initiating a new—if fleeting—type within Britain. I have called this the "triumphal type," for its reliance on the forms of Roman triumphal arches, all monumental arches and appliquéd sculptural decoration. The new builders saw bridges as appropriate settings for architectural ornament: a mighty contrast with the restrained form of Westminster Bridge, which can barely be said to have a style at all.[71] If Westminster, taken at face value, is a work of almost pure engineering, most of the myriad designs for Blackfriars are works of engineered architecture, bearing the trappings of traditional buildings and monuments—columns and loggie, entablatures, sculpture—but reusing them in a new fashion.[72] Although the various triumphal entries for the Blackfriars competition display a range of features, their collective mining of classical grandeur allows them to be seen as a stylistic group. They were classical showpieces, meant to stand as singular monuments to both their designers' architectural talent and their erudition and familiarity with the ornaments of the antique world. Chambers's aedicules and trophies, Gwynn's domes and festooned spandrels, and even Mylne's double-columned cutwaters— all convey a Roman sense, bridges dressed in the garments of antiquity.[73] Indeed, Mylne's original design, amended when costs overran, contained

statues honoring naval victories, reinforcing the sense of the bridges as triumphal arches for a latter day.[74]

It would be foolish to suggest a single source for the triumphal type, but due credit must be given to Giovanni Battista Piranesi, whose 1750 engraving for a *ponte magnifico* surely inspired the lavish, overwrought, classically ornamented designs of Gwynn, Chambers, and Adam. Piranesi's 1756 publication of *Le antichità Romane* must have also provided the aspirant designers with ideas on how to pilfer the remains of Roman antiquity.[75] Though Piranesi was not an entrant in the Blackfriars competition himself (he was in Italy), his forms, as expressed in his *ponte magnifico*, reappear again and again in the competitors' designs. While Piranesi's chunky, colonnaded classicism permeates the Blackfriars designs, there was something broader at work in the rise of the triumphal type—something akin to the contemporaneous rise of the English landscape garden. While the naturalistic gardens were, for patrons, "happy memories of the Italian landscape as experienced on the Grand Tour," the triumphal bridge designs must have functioned as similar souvenirs of the architects' experiences sketching in the remains of the antique world.[76]

LEFT: Giovanni Battista Piranesi, *Ponte magnifico ...* , *ca.* 1750. Piranesi's "ponte magnifico" inspired the lavish, overwrought, classically ornamented designs of the Blackfriars Bridge competition.

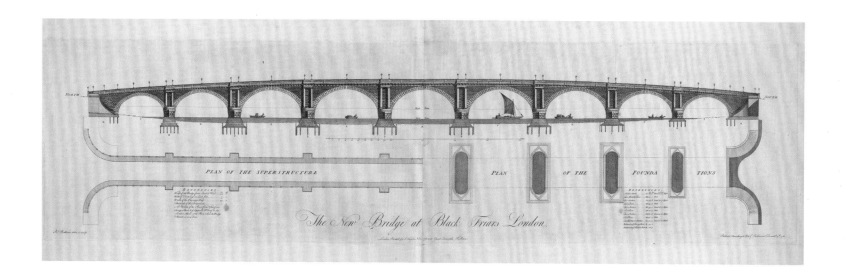

PLAN OF THE SUPERSTRUCTURE   PLAN   OF THE   FOUNDA   TIONS

The New Bridge at Black Friars London.

Mylne's Blackfriars is an unfussy design: "modest without bordering on rusticity";
as in Jones's St. Paul's, only the barest ornament was permitted

Mylne's entry was apparently chosen for the way it pared down the excesses of the triumphal type while still nodding at them with each pier bearing twin columns.[77] His own justification for his design confirms this; he claims that the bridge's "particular parts ... are all dictated by utility, and by becoming ornaments render it very much in the simple and genuine taste of Covent-Garden church."[78] Mylne relates his theory of bridge building, whereby useful elements comprise the only ornaments, to Inigo Jones's St. Paul's Covent Garden, the so-called

"handsomest barn in England." Mylne's Blackfriars is an unfussy design: "modest without bordering on rusticity"; as in Jones's St. Paul's, only the barest ornament was permitted, nothing to distract from the structure's fundamental utility.[79] While this synthetic approach to the triumphal type was Mylne's great achievement, the attempted subjugation of the ornamental columns to structural elements of the piers—like Jones's Tuscan order holding up the St. Paul's portico—does not quite come off. Labelye's Westminster Bridge compellingly omitted columns of any

ABOVE: Mylne's entry paired down the excesses of the triumphal type while still nodding at them. Robert Baldwin, *The New Bridge, Blackfriars, London*, 1766. OPPOSITE: Mylne claimed the bridge's elements were "all dictated by utility". William Marlow, *St. Paul's and Blackfriars Bridge*, between 1770 and 1772.

sort, proving the appeal of such a design. Mylne, however much he sought to reduce the classical ornament on his design for Blackfriars Bridge, could not avoid the urge to display his classical learning. This was not lost on John Smeaton, the prolific bridge builder and civil engineer, who, in 1760, directly rebutted Mylne's pamphlet's criticism of his design with a pamphlet of his own. Mylne, as Publicus, had written that Smeaton's entry was the "meanest and poorest of all."[80] In his response, Smeaton takes aim at the overabundance of ornament of Mylne's design, specifically the columned piers: "as the ancient orders are not applicable to bridges as such, ornaments borrowed therefrom have always been used very sparingly."[81] Smeaton's design, its only ornament the domes topping each pier, diverges from the triumphal type in recalling Labelye's Westminster Bridge: emphasizing the structure's inherent function rather than serving as a showpiece design to be viewed in isolation.

Robert Adam was clearly uneasy about the Blackfriars competition, but he almost certainly submitted designs. In 1988 Damie Stillman identified three drawings in the Soane Museum as Adam's likely entry into the Blackfriars competition.[82] Part of Adam's difficulties surrounding the Blackfriars project may come from personal antipathy to Robert Mylne. Adam had always been suspicious of Mylne, from their time spent contemporaneously in Rome, but Mylne's Blackfriars commission seems to have engendered further animosity. Of the brothers Mylne, Adam wrote: "They have neither money nor education to make themselves known to strangers ... few people know there are such lads in Rome, but as they apply very closely and will undoubtedly make considerable progress, one does not know what may be the consequence with the fickle, new-fangled, ignorant Scotch nobles and gentles who may prefer them to people of more taste and judgement."[83] Robert's brother James

was particularly dismissive of Mylne, referring to him only as "Blackfriars" and remarking in 1761 in a letter to Robert that "Blackfriars was at school with me and he now throws a bridge over the Thames and the world approves of his skill."[84] A particularly telling episode occurred in 1762, when, according to James, a guest of the Abbé Peter Grant—priest to the Scottish in Rome—insisted that Mylne was the "ablest architect in Britain" on the evidence that "Bob Adam gave in his designs for the *ponte* and those of Mylne were preferred." Grant denied that Robert had submitted designs, such an attempt being "beneath his character and importance," but the man insisted. Grant, defensive of the Adams, disparaged his guest as a "madman," "cyclops," and a "dwarf," and his bellicosity may suggest how interested he was in suppressing the truth that Robert *had* in fact submitted designs.[85] Not having won the competition, he thereafter thought it better to obscure his personally embarrassing defeat by claiming he had never entered at all, perhaps mortified at losing to a man who had walked to Rome to undertake his grand tour, rather than traveling in a chariot.[86]

Adam's design, if we accept that it is for the Blackfriars competition, is situated, stylistically, between Gwynn's flamboyant entry and Mylne's comparatively sober one.[87] The bridge is of nine round arches with a gentle gradient rising toward the center; each pier includes an aedicule populated by a statue, bearing the names Pitt, Boscawen, George II, and George Prince of Wales.[88] The cutwaters are capped by diagonal crowns; the spandrels bear paterae. Swag-and-patera paneling, scrolls, and fluted friezes sit below the balustrade, while reclining figures sit above the central arch's piers. A busy design, Adam's bridge is an academic exercise in translating Piranesi's *ponte magnifico* into an English idiom; he would adopt some of the design's features in a more restrained manner for an unbuilt design at Kedleston two years later.[89]

LEFT: Likely Robert Adam's entry into the Blackfriars Bridge competition: a busy design he later avoided mentioning.

Design of a Bridge for The Right...
Over a Fall of Water fronting His...
Span of the Arch...

urable The Lord Scarsdale; Proposed to be Built

ps House at Kedleston in Derbyshire.

. . . from Column to Column 190 Feet

ABOVE: A bridge designed for Kedleston Hall, Derbyshire, 1761.
Here Adam took features of his Blackfriars entry and pared them
down to a scale more appropriate for a private commission.

Bridges in the mid-eighteenth century attained the status of major public works, representative of the aspirational improving impulse, and were celebrated as such. Indicative of this is the popularity of "views" of the London crossings in prints, drawings, and paintings. Canaletto made more than ten drawings or paintings of Westminster Bridge alone, while Edward Rooker produced a popular print of Blackfriars in the process of construction—a testament to the physical process of improvement.[90] Celebration of the improving triumphal bridge may have reached its zenith with Thomas Sandby's "Bridge of Magnificence," a fantasia illustrated for his final Royal Academy lecture in 1760.[91] Made just after the Blackfriars competition, Sandby's sixteen-foot drawing is the logical conclusion of the triumphal-bridge trend, incorporating whole, regular, and classically ornamented buildings atop the span with a loggia between them. The thick piers serve as rusticated ground-floor frontages for the buildings above, taking the edifice metaphor further by including sash windows—this is a superstructure in the guise of a bridge. Such a bridge was never built, nor could be feasibly, but the widespread acceptance of its appropriateness was affirmed by the 1781 exhibition of the drawing at the Royal Academy,

where one observer commented that the design was so sublime that "the Motion for it, in the House of Commons, should originate with Mr *Burke*," playing off the title of the parliamentarian and philosopher Edmund Burke's 1757 treatise, *A Philosophical Enquiry into the Origin of Our Ideas of the Sublime and Beautiful*.[92] John Soane's 1776 illustration of a bridge for a Royal Academy lecture, went even further in creating almost a miniature city atop a bridge.

Robert Adam never produced a bridge of magnificence, but he approached the idea in his Pulteney Bridge, designed 1770, and much later in his proposed designs for Edinburgh's New Town crossings. He was to begin his bridge-building career in earnest on a smaller scale, as part of the estate improvements to which he contributed in the 1760s.

Ultimately, Adam's bridge work proves an illuminating topic for the way it touches on so many aspects of his practice. A fusion of his early engineering experience, his longstanding interest in the picturesque, his sense of monumentality, and his experimentation with various styles, his bridge building is reflective of his immense talent and the wide scope of his interests. In conceiving of bridges as part of what Ranald MacInnes has called a "doctrine of architectural totality," Adam eschewed the more common approach to bridges as singular monuments to their makers, so evident in triumphal-type bridges and bridges of magnificence.[93] Indeed, while his fellow architects designed bridges as decorated skeletons, Adam's approach was directly opposed. As he stated in his 1773 publication of his *Works in Architecture*, a bridge must be built from the "ideas which naturally arise in beholding the adjacent scenes."[94] This was to be his guiding principle: that bridges must be contextually appropriate, not isolated monuments; his work on estates, public bridges, and even unbuilt schemes bears this out.

PART OF THE BRIDGE AT BLACKFRIARS.

LEFT: Engineering to the fore—a testament to the physical process of improvement. Edward Rooker, *Part of the Bridge at Blackfriars*, 1777. OPPOSITE: One of many Canaletto views of Westminster Bridge—a resplendent monument. Canaletto, *Westminster Bridge, with the Lord Mayor's Procession on the Thames*, 1747.

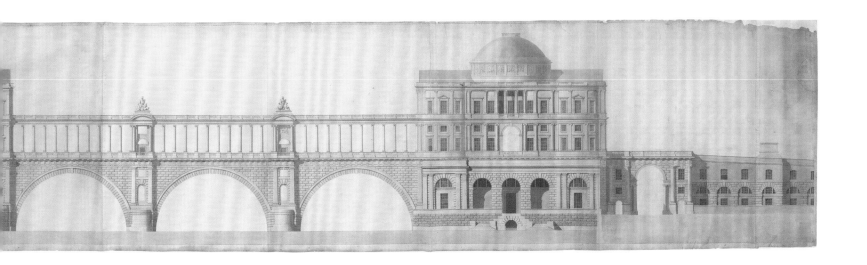

TOP: A triumphal bridge approaching the sublime. Thomas Sandby, *Bridge of Magnificence*, 1755. OPPOSITE: Soane's triumphal bridge scheme may have gone further than any other. Office of Sir John Soane, *Design for a Triumphal Bridge*: A watercolor of the design made in 1776 for which Soane won the Gold Medal at the Royal Academy. Dated July 19, 1799 and drawn by Joseph Gandy. ABOVE: Paul Sandby, *Design for a Bridge near Somerset Place, ca.* 1780.

CHAPTER III

Robert Adam's Estate Bridges

Robert Adam's earliest direct exposure to the practice of architecture was at Fort George, where he and his brother James supervised construction in the early 1750s.[95] Although they did not design what was built there, including the surrounding rampart walls, the experience must have made a strong impression on the brothers. While Robert Adam's bridges approach a fortified style only when conforming to existing fortified structures, this early exposure to the necessities of masonry must have contributed to his ability to design credible, structurally sound bridges, his skill as what we would now call an engineer.[96]

Adam surely learned something of bridge building from his father and brothers. William Adam's bridge at Aberfeldy provided him with an attractive model: Adam continuously returned to the design of a parapet that sweeps down at the sides. Though the Aberfeldy bridge is more mannered—with its obelisks and quoins—than most of Robert's built designs, its blocky masonry aspects and use of ornament provided him an early standard. The bridge at Dumfries House and the two at Inveraray Castle offered Robert a sense of the way bridges could be manipulated for their picturesque potential or made to hint at the style to come.[97] The

Dumfries bridge was built to give the visitor an early view of the approaching house and its central balustrade previews the nearly identical one at the house's front steps.[98] Robert Adam almost always used bridges as stylistic previews of the houses to which they led: a lesson clearly learned from, or perhaps with, John.[99] Bolstered by a family tradition of bridge building, Adam applied this knowledge to his own practice, creating distinguished estate bridges that exploited picturesque possibilities and added to stylistic cohesion within the estate's architectural totality.

Audley End

Adam's initial solo exercise in bridge building was at Mitcham Grove, in Surrey, near the English capital to which he had recently moved. Merely wooden crossings over small streams, the bridges Adam designed for Archibald Stewart depressed Adam, who groused to his brother James, "On such pityfull Objects is my attention bent."[100] Such trifles were frustrating to the ambitious Adam, whose real aims were monumental public projects, or at least works greater than wooden footbridges. His

OPPOSITE: The bridge over the River Cam at Audley End, Essex, gives a preview of the house.

wishes were fulfilled at Audley End around 1763. Already employed in the redecoration of Audley End House, he was concomitantly commissioned to carry out improvements to the estate's built environment—a pattern that was to repeat itself throughout his career. John Griffin Griffin inherited the house in 1762 and immediately began an extensive program of improvement, both within the Jacobean house and on its extensive grounds. The total cost of these enhancements and amendments to the house and grounds reached £100,000, an enormous sum for the day.[101]

Adam's work on the house's grounds coincided with Griffin Griffin's retention of Lancelot "Capability" Brown to remodel the existing formal gardens into a coherent vision of the new "English landscape" style.[102] Brown's work at Audley End was characteristic of his famed method, and as elsewhere he refashioned Audley End to include a "wide sweeping lawn and sunken fence allowing unbroken vision from the house" in addition to the "artfully scattered clumps of trees and the serpentine river."[103] Mirroring the aesthetic improvement of the gardens—the opening up of views, the sweeping away of formal parterres, the construction of follies—was a program of practical improvement. Partitioned estates were

combined, and streets were moved off the principal lawns.[104] Moreover, "roads were levelled, widened and gravelled," and all these works were dually beneficial, both increasing the productivity of the estate and beautifying it.[105] Complementing Brown's efforts was Adam's program of garden architecture, including the construction in 1763 of a bridge over the River Cam, newly widened and made irregular by Brown.

A new bridge connecting the house to the London–Walden road was part of Griffin Griffin's original plans for Audley End's improvement.[106] Like Brown's improving work in the gardens, the bridge had a twofold benefit: practically allowing visitors to reach the house and aesthetically improving the vista of the main approach. The first drawing of the bridge gives a complete sense of Adam's intentions.[107] Three segmental arches rise gently, the central being the largest, with two piers sunk into the river itself and two piers on the banks. The balustraded parapet contains quatrefoil piercings above the piers, which accord with the Jacobean exterior of the house, visible from the bridge's crossing. The rusticated, diagonally jutting cutwaters add solidity to an otherwise light bridge; these correspond with the cutwaters depicted in Adam's designs for Blackfriars. The parapet sweeps angularly down over the outer piers, echoing that on William Adam's 1733 bridge at Aberfeldy.[108] As built, the Audley End bridge lost some of its elegance: it is lower to the ground, sturdier, and lacking the "Aberfeldy profile" of the design. The later removal of the quatrefoils from the parapet robbed the bridge of some of its connection to the house but allowed it to cohere better with the neoclassicism of subsequent garden buildings. Adam later designed two eye-catchers for the garden: a "Grecian Temple" (designed 1763, built 1771) to sit atop a hill on the estate, and an obelisk (designed 1763)—both of which help to explain the 1781 alteration of the bridge's parapet.[109]

LEFT: General Wade's Bridge, Aberfeldy, Scotland, built in 1733 by William Adam, which provided Robert Adam with an early model for bridge building. OPPOSITE: Adam's original design for the entrance bridge at Audley End was meant to harmonize with the Jacobean house.

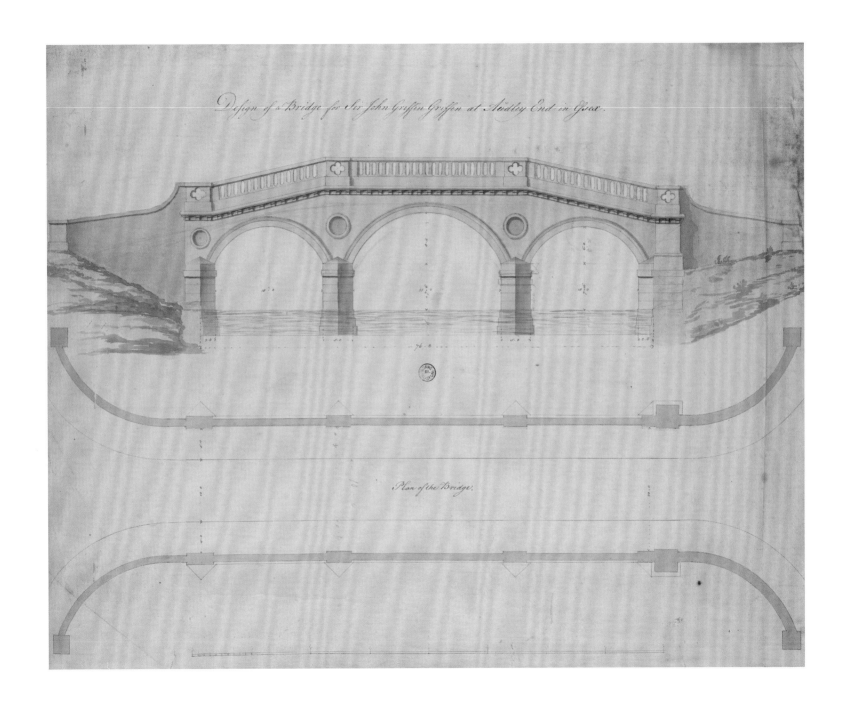

Design of a Bridge for Sir John Griffin Griffin at Audley End in Essex.

Plan of the Bridge.

The bridge's positioning determined its initial design. Built as the major feature of the direct route to the Jacobean house, the bridge was meant to frame the house just as the house frames the bridge; the visual interplay between the two functions more convincingly if the two are stylistically sympathetic. But as the garden increased in importance, the bridge was remodeled to accord with the new and prominent garden structures. Whereas the bridge was, at first, a hint of the Jacobean house that comes into view across its span, it later became a reference to the expensive modern garden.

Adam's stylistic malleability is evident in his second bridge project at Audley End, the Palladian "tea-house" designed in 1782. Again crossing the River Cam, this time at a comparatively short span, the tea-house bridge is a folly that happens to cross a river. It stands as a single segmental arch, piers on the banks, with a three-bay Ionic portico above it, the frieze housing face roundels, with a dentil entablature and a central raised panel over the cornice—a fitting adornment to Brown's neoclassical garden. The tea-house is a fashionable indulgence, one without equivalent in Adam's oeuvre, owing to its miniature size and mannered decoration. It belongs to a mid-eighteenth-century tradition of "Palladian" bridge building begun by Henry Herbert, ninth Earl of Pembroke, who worked with the architect Roger Morris to construct the first Palladian garden bridge at Wilton House in 1736–37.[110] These designs, directly based on Palladian antecedents from the *Quattro Libri* or adopting a similar idiom, were built as part of grounds improvements through the 1740s, '50s, and '60s, at Hagley, Wotton, and Prior Park.[111] Adam assented to the fashionable style of the Palladian garden bridge but modified it in keeping with his general approach to bridge building.[112] The designers of standard Palladian bridges treated them as monuments to classical erudition, stuffing as

much ornament as possible within small frames, like at Wilton, where the bridge bears rusticated spandrels, loggia, and dueling pedimented lodges. Adam modified the form by reducing the Palladian bridge to its barest outlines, just a colonnaded summerhouse open on three sides with a wrought-iron railing rather than a full balustrade sitting above barely decorated spandrels. Adam's antipathy towards Palladio, that "blackguard," whom he sought to "attack ... sword in hand," may have informed his rejection of the ostentatiously Palladian bridges then popular in the English landscape garden.[113] While most Palladian bridge builders were

ABOVE: Lower to the ground and sturdier, the bridge as built lost some of its elegance. OPPOSITE, LEFT: The Palladian Bridge at Wilton House. OPPOSITE, RIGHT: The "tea-house" bridge at Audley End: a folly that happens to cross a river.

concerned with creating decontextualized monuments, Adam attended to the way his tea-house bridge would fit within the greater scene at Audley End. Visible from his original bridge, the tea-house bridge needed to accord with the panorama; unlike other Palladian bridges it could not stand as a singular monument, something Adam realized in his design.

Alnwick Castle

As at Audley End, Adam's bridge work at Alnwick Castle was part of a comprehensive program of improvement (internal and external), and again he fit his design within the scope and style of the existing built environment.[114] Beginning work at the house in 1769, he redecorated seven rooms internally in a "Gothic" style, likely at the request of the Duchess of Northumberland, who manifested a serious interest in Gothic decoration, as opposed to her husband, whose tastes ran more to conventional neoclassicism.[115] The work, which coincided with the Percy family's move of its main seat from Syon to Alnwick, seems to have been motivated by the Duchess's profound feeling for ancestry.[116] Alnwick had been occupied by Percys since 1309 and had served defensive purposes in the fifteenth and sixteenth centuries.[117] A sense of this legacy, combined with the Duchess's sensitivity to the new Gothic styles appearing in fashionable places—in 1762 she said she had "never seen anything as pretty as Strawberry Hill"—led to a major program of "gothicization" at the house and grounds.[118] As at Audley End and also at Syon—where Adam had previously worked for the Northumberlands in the early 1760s—the improvement program involved "Capability" Brown, who was brought in to refurbish the house's grounds and gardens.[119] Adam's collaboration with Brown on the landscape is difficult to untangle, but he seems to have had a hand in building and renovating multiple structures there.

The two most identifiable remnants of Adam's work at Alnwick are the "Lion Bridge" and the "Brislee Tower," both enthusiastic forays into what might be called a "garden gothick" style. The Lion Bridge stands as the most elaborate major bridge Adam ever designed for an estate.[120] Crossing the river Aln, and replacing a previous bridge on the site that

OPPOSITE: Battlements for both: Alnwick Castle seen from the Lion Bridge. ABOVE: William Beilby (1740–1819), *Bridge at Alnwick Castle, Northumberland.*

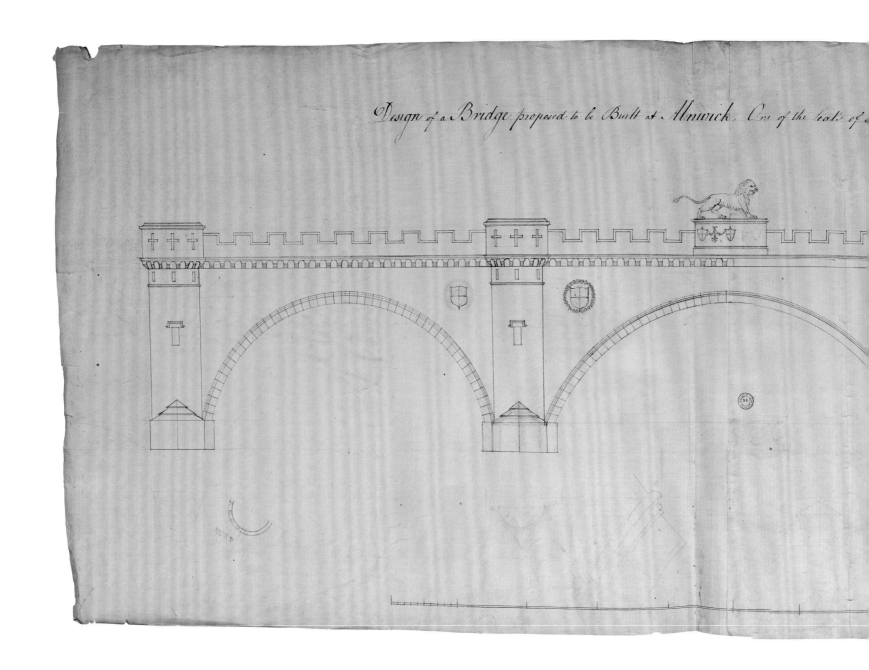

Design of a Bridge proposed to be Built at Alnwick, One of the Seats of ...

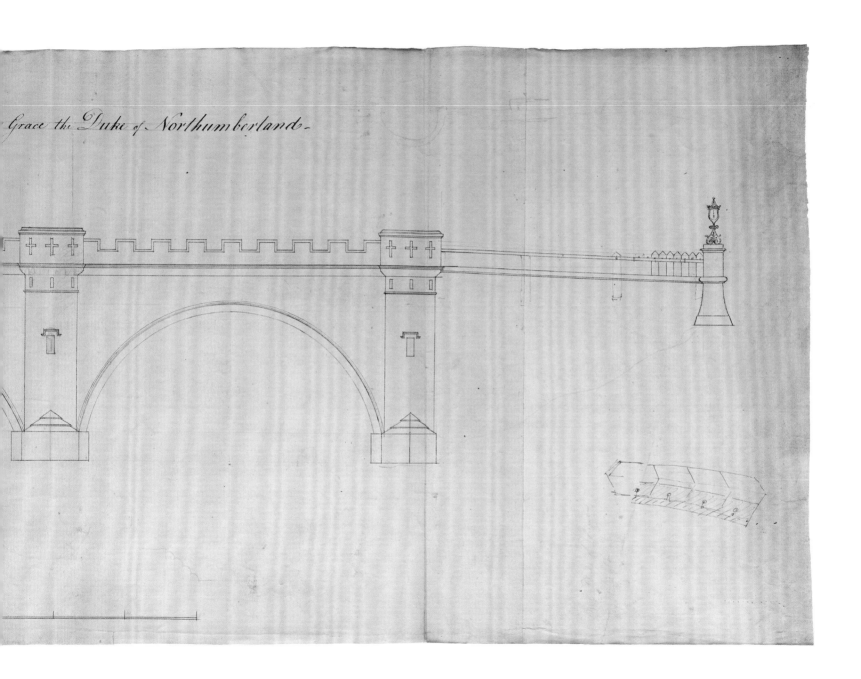

Grace the Duke of Northumberland.

Adam attended to the details, too, by designing the "approach walls" in the "form of sharpened palings reproduced in stone"

had washed away in the floods of 1771, it leads visitors from the north directly to the castle's entrance.[121] The bridge comprises three substantial segmental arch spans, the piers as projecting half-cylinder turrets, pierced at the top by arrowslits in the form of crosses fronting embrasures. Rather than the balustraded parapets so common in Adam's other bridges, the Lion Bridge is appropriately crenellated, matching the house's battlements. Underneath the parapet are decorative machicolations and rusticated spandrels with shields, while above a sculpted Percy lion completes the castle air, standing like a central shield, complementing the house's interior heraldic elements.[122] Adam attended to the details, too, by designing the "approach walls" in the "form of sharpened palings reproduced in stone —a veritable petrified stockade."[123] The bridge matches what Laura Mayer

The details work to reinforce what John Vanbrugh called, in another context, the "castle air." PREVIOUS SPREAD: Robert Adam's original drawing for the Lion Bridge at Alnwick, *ca.* 1770–73

calls the castle's "compelling bloody history," and the Northumberlands' promotion of this overarching agenda surely directed Adam's approach to the design.[124] Later viewers of the bridge recognized its essential relation to the house. Consider J. M. W. Turner's *circa* 1829 watercolor *Alnwick Castle*, which depicts the bridge in the foreground and the castle in the back.[125] As Turner has it, the bridge and the castle are a single unit, working together to create a single castellated impression. In the painting, the bridge's turrets lead our eye to the castle's turrets, just as they do in real life—confirmation that Adam's scenographic approach was understood just as well in the decades after he pioneered it as it is now. Turner even plays a slight trick on the viewer to suggest the close association of bridge and castle, which is to tinker with the perspective, making the bridge and castle appear much closer than they are. In real life it is quite a steep climb up the Peth to reach the castle, which sits high on the hill, but Turner recognized that the picturesque possibilities could be exploited further by linking the two structures even more closely in his painting than they are in real life. These picturesque qualities are only heightened by Turner's decision to depict the scene at night, with a luminous central moon providing the light source, creating a shimmer on the river Aln and imparting a spectral quality to the stags who graze on the bank.[126]

As at Audley End, Adam worked at Alnwick within the existing setting to produce an elegant but not grandiose structure meant to harmonize with the style of the house and remodeled grounds: rather than impose a monumental, isolated design, he preferred to complement the existing architecture and environment. His other architectural contributions to these programs bear this out. At Audley End he was responsible for the circular temple of 1771, a fittingly neoclassical structure for an English landscape garden; at Alnwick the Brislee Tower, though

ALNWICK CASTLE.

OPPOSITE: Turner understood Adam's picturesque intentions perfectly. J.M.W. Turner (born London 1775; died Chelsea [London] 1851), *Alnwick Castle*, ca.1829, London. Watercolour on paper, 29.0 x 42.9 cm. South Australian Government Grant 1958, Art Gallery of South Australia, Adelaide, 0.1814.
ABOVE: The combined view of bridge and castle quickly became canonical. William Le Petit, *Alnwick Castle the Seat of the Right Honorable Hugh Percy*, early 1800s.

more fantastical than the Lion Bridge, fits within the scope of the consciously historicizing and medievalizing renovations undertaken by the Northumberlands. Adam's achievement in estate-bridge building was to eschew highly personal architectural expressions—instead concentrating on the possibilities of bridges to serve as parts of a greater architectural scheme. Adam exploited the bridges' potential as viewing platforms: he knew visitors would look from the bridges directly to the houses, and thereby sought to create harmony between the two landscape elements. While other bridge builders created bridges specifically meant to be viewed alone, Adam built bridges to be viewed in context, as constituent elements of a greater prospect. A bridge designed in accordance with architectural or landscape features is even more powerful for the way it can allude to those features.

Adam's approach to estate bridges owes a clear debt to classical landscape paintings of the sort perfected by Claude Lorrain, with whose work he was familiar.[127] The library at Blair Adam, where Adam spent countless hours sketching, included a folio of picturesque engravings after Gaspard Dughet and Claude; also in the library was a folio of drawings by Adam after these engravings.[128] Given the predominance of bridges in the two artists' work, it is certain that Adam internalized both the conventional segmental-arch form of these masonry bridges and the way they could be exploited for their picturesque possibilities: serving as links between landscape and architecture. In a Claudian landscape picture, the observer can both view the bridge as a part of the landscape ensemble and project himself moving over the bridge, progressing from landscape, to bridge, to building—something Adam understood and articulated consistently in his bridge-building projects. These wispy landscapes of gently curving rivers, rustic bridges, and ruined castles had a major influence on the rise of the English landscape garden.

RIGHT: The viewer progresses from landscape to bridge to building.

If one considers a typical Claudian landscape, such as the 1645 *Pastoral Landscape with the Ponte Molle*, it is easy to see how Adam could conceive of his estate bridges as architectural realizations of these parts of Claude's canvases.[129] To the right a masonry bridge with segmental arches crosses a river, leading from one shore to another, drawing the viewer's eye to the medieval Italian buildings at left. The square, turreted towers and crenellated lodge reference the fortified nature of the circular tower in the foreground at left. The bridge is integral to the scenographic logic of the painting: it not only leads the eye to the cluster of buildings but also achieves a stylistic harmony with them. It is this effect that Adam attempted to achieve at Audley End, Alnwick, and in his other estate bridges. The bridge served as both a stylistic reference to the house to come and a natural point of procession, drawing the visitor in. He thereby used the dual possibilities of the bridge, as a part of the greater landscape—to be viewed from afar—and as an essential part of the house's architectural entirety, the first place a visitor could get a sense of the approaching building.

Later views of Audley End and Alnwick confirm Adam's conception of the bridge as part of a Claudian landscape made real. In a painting of Audley End by Edmund Garvey, *circa* 1782, the first Adam bridge stands in the foreground, leading the viewer's eye to the house behind. As with the Turner watercolor of Alnwick, the house needs the bridge—as a practical roadway, but also as a stylistic reference, a frontispiece for what is to come. That painters often picked up on the picturesque potential of Adam's estate bridges can be no coincidence. Adam understood the multiple ways bridges could function in relation to houses and landscapes and created bridges that served as convincing, attractive parts of built compositions.

ABOVE: A classical and classic scene displaying the pictoral logic Adam later applied to his bridges. Claude Lorrain, *Landscape near Rome with a View of the Ponte Molle*, 1645.
OPPOSITE: The house needs the bridge. Edmund Garvey, *View of Audley End from the West*, 1782.

The Pulteney Bridge, Bath

Robert Adam's Pulteney Bridge, designed in 1770 at the behest of William Johnstone Pulteney to connect Bath and the then-undeveloped suburb of Bathwick, stands alone in his oeuvre. Though Adam was consistently engaged with public bridge projects throughout his career, starting with the Blackfriars competition in 1759, the Pulteney was the only public bridge he built; as such, it is his largest. Even so, it again displays the hallmarks of Adam's bridge work: it was an improving project concerned with matching the prevailing style of its setting, an attempt to capture the overtly, consciously neoclassical style that had predominated in Bath since the 1720s. Despite its monumental appearance, it was built simultaneously to accord with the existing architectural framework of the burgeoning city and to serve as the entrance to a similarly styled suburb to be built to Adam's designs.

The city of Bath was, by the middle of the eighteenth century, engaged in a concerted project of improvement directed by the city's Corporation, a process that took on a decidedly architectural character.[130] In 1706 the Corporation applied to Parliament "for a Power to amend the principal Roads leading to Bath; to pave, cleanse, and light the Streets."[131] An Act of

Parliament was obtained in 1710 to bridge the Avon towards Bristol and a further improvement act was granted in 1720.[132] These acts modernized the city, encouraging the construction of new buildings and the updating of old ones; as the architect John Wood wrote in 1748, "thatch'd Coverings were exchanged to such as were tiled; low and obscure Lights were turned into elegant Sash Windows; and every one was lavish in Ornaments to adorn the Outsides of them, even to Profuseness."[133] Wood himself was responsible for the bulk of the new building, laying out Queen Square (begun 1728), an early example of façadism in English house building, with a unified front belying individual houses within.[134] Queen Square pioneered what would become typical of Bath's eighteenth-century architecture: Bath stone used in the service of a quiet classicism; regular façades adorned with engaged columns; ornament only in the forms of pediment-topped windows and the occasional urn. The dominance of this species of Palladianism was largely owing to the industry of Wood and his son, John Wood the Younger. So compelling was it that other Bath builders appropriated it for considerably more modest developments; surely there is a hint of pride in Wood's dismissal of Beaufort Square—Queen Square rendered in half—as "piratical."[135]

By the time Adam built the Pulteney Bridge, the city's architectural character was secure. Wood the Younger had completed his father's Circus (begun 1754, completed 1768)—an elaboration of the ideas found at Queen Square—and designed the Royal Crescent (begun 1767), another residential monument in the style his father had pioneered.[136] The noticeable stylistic unity in Bath's eighteenth-century architecture is a testament both to the vision of the Woods and to the self-consciously architectural improvements undertaken by the Corporation. The city had intentionally sought to improve its setting, and the Woods provided a replicable architectural approach: "uniformity was reinforced by the repeated use of standardized building forms introduced by the Woods; the Palladian terrace, the palatial façade, and the crescent."[137] Contemporary observers recognized the abundance of new building: the 1753 *Bath and Bristol Guide* posited that "The city of Bath is greatly improved within these few Years, in its Buildings; the new Houses are strong, large, and commodious; built with Free-Stone," while the 1755 revised edition could note that "buildings erected within these few years ... have been very extensive."[138] Remaining medieval buildings—including parish churches—and fortifications were either torn down or modified to accord with the new and much-lauded construction; by mid-century Bath had, "in the name of 'improvement' ... lost irretrievably the majority of its medieval and early modern physical heritage."[139]

When Robert Adam was commissioned to design the Pulteney Bridge, he was a participant in Bath's conscious and directed architectural transformation. Although the delayed development of Bathwick caused the bridge to appear as an isolated monument, it was originally envisioned as an essential part of a new townscape. The idea to bridge the city of Bath to undeveloped Bathwick, just across the Avon to the east of the center of town, originated in the 1750s, years after William Pulteney, the first Earl of Bath, inherited the Bathwick estate. Nothing came of earlier proposals until in 1767 William Johnstone Pulteney, who inherited the

By the time Adam built the Pulteney Bridge, the city's architectural character was secure

OPPOSITE: Thomas Hearne, *View of Bath from Spring Gardens*, 1790.

The bridge as built is Adam's daring attempt to work within Bath's existing Palladian framework

estate through his wife, immediately set about reviving the idea.[140] Johnstone Pulteney was well aware of the commercial potential of his newly acquired land, writing to his wife's estate's trustees in 1769 that "The pump Room must always be considered the center of Bath, and therefore the nearer we can bring our ground to that center, the more valuable it will be for building ... this New Bridge ... will give a short & commodious passage for chairs & persons on foot ... By means of which a good dale [*sic*] of the Bathwick ground will be within a sixpenny fare of the Pump room, playhouse, coffee houses & assembly rooms."[141] Another letter confirms his intention to use the bridge to spur the development of his property: "If a Bridge is built over the Avon somewhere near the City Prison, it is expected that a good deal of the Ground near the Bridge will be taken by Builders for erecting Houses and that they will agree to considerable Ground Rents."[142] It seems that the original idea was to build a bridge and let the builders sort out the rest; to this end he first engaged Thomas Paty of Bristol to produce designs for a simple masonry bridge with three arches. It was this bridge that the Bath Corporation approved.[143]

The scope of the project changed considerably upon Robert Adam's replacement of Paty in 1770. Suddenly the project was for a showpiece bridge with shops to connect to a new town designed by Adam.[144] The bridge as built between 1770 and 1774 is Adam's daring attempt to work within Bath's existing Palladian framework while also leading seamlessly

RIGHT: The Pulteney Bridge, built by Robert Adam between 1770 and 1774, as viewed from the south.

The lodges themselves are pleasing
little structures, essays in a pared-down
classicism, and exceedingly charming

to the new town of Bathwick—Johnstone Pulteney maintained that "it is important to the success of the whole plan that the communication be made not only easy but pleasant."[145] Like the rest of Bath, the Pulteney Bridge was constructed in Bath stone and wears its references to Palladio clearly but not overbearingly. With its central pedimented pavilion, rows of shops, and identical lodges at either end, Adam clearly had Palladio's unexecuted design for Venice's Rialto Bridge in mind.[146] But, following the custom in Bath, Adam simplified Palladio's animated design, eliminating the central portico and the columns applied to the wings radiating off the center. Instead, the bridge presents a Venetian window, the lights of which are set between elegant Doric half-columns, and plain surfaces moving outwards toward the lodges, pierced only by regular sash windows and two pedimented windows. While Palladio's spandrels were rusticated and included aedicules, Adam's are smooth, elaborated only by circular windows over each pier and archivolt moldings on the voussoirs.[147] The lodges themselves are pleasing little structures, essays in a pared-down classicism, and exceedingly charming with their petite domes and recessed arches. The central lodge, which anchors the entirety of the span, is a triumph with its Venetian window, set within a graceful scalloped relieving arch. Adam's usual urge to exuberance is here curbed; the bridge's elaborate form was more than enough.

Even so, Adam's design is rich compared to Paty's, and the Bath Corporation's reaction to it reveals much about contemporary, competing ideas of bridge building. The shops were deemed an impediment on multiple levels: "the circulation of Air will be prevented ... the Smoak will greatly incommode the neighbourhood on each side of the River ... [and] if a concourse of people constantly pass over it, which must be the case before the shops can be of any value, the dimensions of the Bridge will

OPPOSITE: The central pedimented pavilion, rows of shops, and flanking lodges recall Palladio's unexecuted design for Venice's Rialto Bridge, but Adam has adapted the design to Bath's unshowy style.
LEFT: A Venetian window anchors the design.

then be too narrow to make the Passage convenient."[148] Moreover, the Corporation noted that a bridge with shops—like old London Bridge—was decidedly outmoded: "it has been for some years past an uniform practice throughout the Kingdom to avoid and condemn incumbrances of this kind."[149] Yet Adam's concern was not public health or convenience, nor the fashionability of shops, but rather to provide a suitably grand entrance to the proposed new town at Bathwick, one that would conform stylistically with the typical Bath style on the west side of the bridge and his planned designs for the east side. The famous mid-eighteenth-century buildings of Bath and the bridge would even share the same honeyed "Bath" limestone. And though the Corporation thought the shops a dated encumbrance, they were necessary to draw visitors from one side of the river to the other. In a way, the shops give the bridge its purpose, allowing it to serve as the link between built Bath and to-be-built Bathwick.

Adam's proposed buildings at Bathwick were to be massive five-story riverside blocks. In their simple profile—the only embellishment bowed, three-bay pavilions at each end with engaged Corinthian columns—the buildings echo the Pulteney Bridge's discreet and blocky profile. But the buildings—with their engaged columns and sash windows above a course of arches—refer to not only the bridge leading to them, but also to the iconic Bath architectural formation: the crescent. With their gentle curvature, sweeping mildly around the banks of the river, the buildings recall John Wood the Younger's recently constructed Royal Crescent, just across town. While the drawing does not indicate the location of the bridge, the proposed buildings would have been viewable either from the bridge's exit, or viewable as adjacent to the bridge. What is important is not how exactly the two elements would have functioned, but that they were part of the same scheme, visible either in procession or simultaneously.[150]

Because Adam's new town at Bathwick was never built, later viewers of the bridge were deprived of its essential context. John Soane wrote, in a private note to a Royal Academy lecture, that the Pulteney Bridge was "in external appearance disgusting ... The advantage of these bridges, the roadway being nearly level for heavy loaded wagons, is only set off for their want of beauty."[151] In 1864 an observer could say confidently that "it is a real privation that a goodly stream, with its light airs and solemn moods in changeful play, should be put under ground in darkness and display ..."[152] Another, writing in the 1876 edition of *The Original Bath Guide*, noted of the Pulteney Bridge that "but for these erections [the shops], the view from this point would be extremely picturesque, and it is a subject of lasting regret that beauty in this instance was so completely scarified to gain."[153] These denunciations, through no fault of their own, miss the point. The vista intended from the bridge was not of Bath proper, but of Adam's new town, a pendant to the other's elegant architecture. The bridge was to be an integral part of this greater plan. The presence of

Because Adam's new town at Bathwick
was never built, later viewers of the bridge were
deprived of its essential context

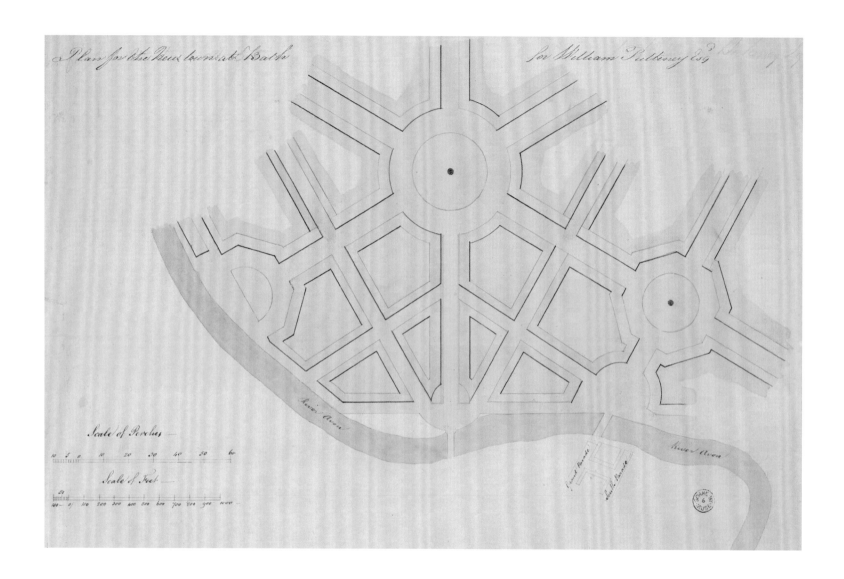

Plan for the New Town at Bath   For William Pulteney Esq

Scale of Perches

Scale of Feet

River Avon

River Avon

ABOVE AND OPPOSITE: Three plans for the buildings at Bathwick,
with the bridge as the central element tying the old town to the new.

three street plans—two dating to 1777 and another to 1782—shows Adam's continuing engagement with the idea of the Pulteney Bridge as the gateway to a bold new town of his design. All three plans show the bridge linking Bath to Bathwick, serving as the main entrance to the new town. Streets radiate axially off the bridge, which in all plans leads directly to a central thoroughfare. Adam clearly conceived of the Pulteney Bridge as a link between the city of Bath—which had been built up so successfully in the previous years—and Bathwick, which, if built, would have complemented the city proper. As the bridge's shops block any view down or upstream, the bridge functions almost as a tunnel, intended to direct observers' gazes towards a massive development at Bathwick, all of which was to be built by Adam. That Thomas Malton immortalized the bridge in a series of drawings just after it was built, all of which portray the bridge as an isolated architectural monument, obscures the way Adam envisioned the bridge. It was to be his contribution to Bath's ongoing project of architectural improvement, a vital and stylistically appropriate link between the Woods' existing edifices and his own new designs. The first Malton view presents Adam's bridge as a triumphal-type bridge, a learned display of classical architecture that just happens to cross a river. The second, though it barely suggests a bridge at all—omitting reference to the river below and the fields on the other side—also presents a decontextualized view, showing only the shops and lodges of the bridge's north side. Malton cannot be blamed for failing to place Adam's bridge in its necessary context—as a stylistically appropriate linkage between old Bath and new Bathwick—since Bathwick had not been built by at the time of the prints' productions. But that he could so compellingly present the Pulteney Bridge as an isolated triumphal-type monument shows the commonplace nature of that conception of bridges. Robert Adam, by desiring to build contextualized bridges as part of larger architectural compositions, was an outlier for the time.

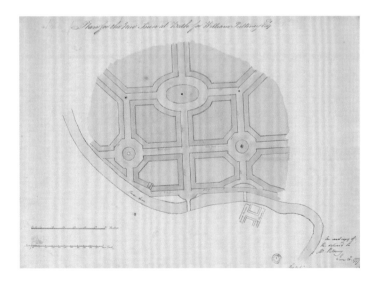

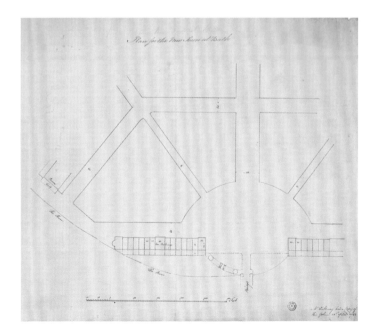

OPPOSITE: Thomas Malton Jr., *Pulteney Bridge, Bath, from the River*, 1785. A triumphal-type bridge decontextualized by the failure of the Bathwick scheme. ABOVE: Thomas Malton Jr., *Pulteney Bridge, Bath*, 1777. This view barely suggests a bridge at all.

CHAPTER V

Built and Unbuilt Visions

Culzean Castle: A Built Vision

Robert Adam's conception of bridges as not merely works of engineered architecture or monumental objects, but as part of larger compositions or tableaux, is borne out by the sheer number of his picturesque drawings that include bridges.[154] These landscapes follow what A. A. Tait called "immutable laws," comprising "endless variations in the relationships and moods of the following elements—the castle, the river with waterfall or loch, the bridge, the causeway bearing figures leading from the foreground to it."[155] The drawings were the products of a more personal side of Adam's multifarious practice: an expression of escapism from the tedium of building elevations made in the Adam office, they "existed to stimulate [his] response to an essential partnership between landscape and architecture."[156] While the Adam office employed a team of highly skilled professional draftsmen, whose major work was to polish Robert's initial sketches for projects, the picturesque drawings are mostly Robert's own work.[157] That so many of these drawings include bridges shows the place they occupied for Adam, as fundamental parts of an architectural and/or landscaped tableau, not isolated monuments. These capricious drawings confirm the built realities visible at Audley End and Alnwick, as well as in Bath. In a way, they provided Adam a way to work out design issues—Tait suggests that they served "as an imaginative quarry to be mined at a variety of levels," and this metaphor applies equally to the bridges shown in them.[158] The finish of these "picturesque" bridges varies widely: some are no more than bare outlines while others are presented in nearly fully worked-up perspectival drawings. The bridges all, however, afforded Adam an opportunity to play with elements for inclusion in his built designs, and furthermore to consider how those elements could be combined in novel ways, always attending to the necessities of the greater composition.

One example, whereby forms used in a picturesque bridge were adapted to a constructed project, illustrates the point. In the National Galleries of Scotland's collection is a watercolor entitled "An Italianate Bridge with Twin Towers," dated *circa* 1780. In it a massive masonry bridge rises over a rocky river flowing through a mountain pass. The bridge's form is, at first glance, unlike anything Adam ever constructed.

OPPOSITE: A picturesque composition from 1774 drawn in connection with Adam's work at Osterley Park. Adam used these sketches to work out ideas and try out details. The house framed by a bridge was a repeated motif in Adam's work both imagined and executed.

OPPOSITE: Robert Adam, *Kirkdale House, Kirkcudbright, Scotland,*
ca. 1786; The so-called "red castle" drawing was sketched in 1786 in
connection with Adam's work at Kirkdale House. The bridge is functional
here, reminiscent of the early Wade bridges he saw on his way to the
Highlands. ABOVE: Robert Adam, *An Italianate Bridge with Twin Towers,*
ca. 1780, National Galleries of Scotland. Drawings like this informed
both his planning and his ornamentation at Culzean and elsewhere.

Four piers are visible, the outermost taking the form of castellated square turrets, with the inner two standing as towers with shallow conical roofs above windowed drums. The outer two arches are tall and semicircular, the center segmental and with a wider span. All three arches have prominently rusticated voussoirs, giving a sense of visual coherence to their disparate forms. The towers contain machicolations and further piercings, reminiscent of the Lion Bridge at Alnwick, while the turrets are also pierced. Above the center arch sits a rectangular panel, again recalling the lion-topped one at Alnwick.

The similarities, however superficial, to the earlier, realized bridge at Alnwick obscure the fact that the 1780 watercolor is an unprecedented design, unlike anything Adam had constructed. With its alternating turret/tower, castellated/Italianate arrangement, it is very much the architectural caprice, an exercise of imagination—Adam never built, nor was commissioned to build, anything so redolent of the Italian *campagna*. This characterization, however, underplays the way in which Adam used these watercolors. Just as Adam explored fanciful designs in his watercolor castles, elements of which were to later be found in erected buildings, he extracted ideas and elements from his watercolor bridges to be used in his built versions. Components of the Italianate design of *circa* 1780 relate to several contained within his "ruined" viaduct at Culzean Castle, the drawing for which dates to 1780. The viaduct surmounts a piece of

uneven land and served as the main drive to the castle.[159] Although a viaduct is not a bridge *per se*, it operates in the same conceptual framework, affording passage over an otherwise unsurmountable span. The presence or absence of water is not essential for something to function just like a bridge. Like the Italianate design, the Culzean viaduct contains towers and turrets, a central segmental arch surrounded by taller, thinner semicircular ones, machicolations, and heavily rusticated voussoirs. But Adam uses the Italianate design merely as a starting point; he extends the irregularity suggested by the watercolor's composition, wherein the bridge appears asymmetrical because of the position of trees, into a design for Culzean that is actually asymmetrical. There Adam fully commits to irregularity, with unevenly spaced arches and non-repeated details like a door arch in one of the central towers but not the other. He mined his watercolor sketch for details to be adapted and expanded in an actual design. While the Italianate design existed in an imaginary landscape, the Culzean viaduct was built to lead directly to the castle-style fantasy house, framing the approach and reflecting the Castle's own appearance. As in all his bridge designs, Adam was careful to match the style of the bridge to that of the house and grounds; Culzean, the seat of Clan Kennedy, was no exception. The watercolor source allows a glimpse into the creative process at work, whereby elements could be drawn out of a sketch and molded into a buildable design.

Adam fully commits to irregularity ... The watercolor source allows
a glimpse into the creative process at work, whereby elements could be drawn out
of a sketch and molded into a buildable design

OPPOSITE: The original design for the Culzean viaduct, dating to 1780, matches closely the executed version.

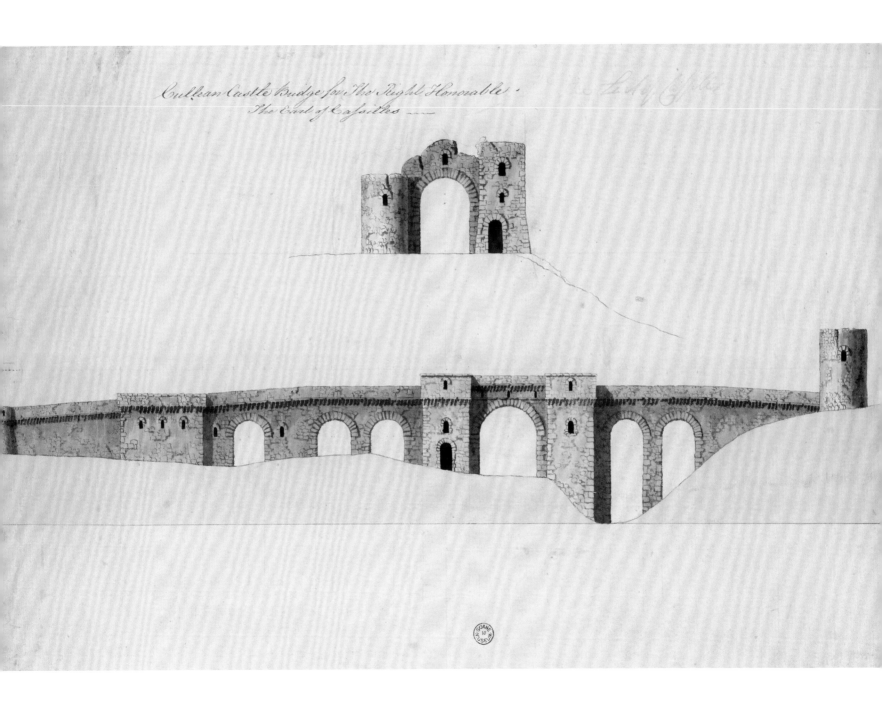

Culzean Castle Bridge for The Right Honorable.
The Earl of Cassilles

Fully integrated into the house, it is an essential element of the architectural tableau. One begins at the ruined arch, through which a view of the house is neatly framed, almost making the massive structure appear small. On a ruined tower is a blind arch, then a functional one at ground level, allowing for a gatekeeper and referring to the arches that recur on the house's principal façade. The entrance arch appears to be falling down, deliberately suggesting antiquity where there is none. But while the house appears straight-on, the path does not. The parapet angles jaggedly, leading the visitor on a twisted route, thereby offering multiple views of the house, from multiple angles, creating a sense of anticipation. The refuges along the way are like bartizans, implying fortification in what is essentially a decorative structure. As one processes, the house comes more clearly into view, showing its decorative elements, especially the arrowslit-style cross windows that are echoed by the actual arrowslits in the tower at the end of the viaduct, all adding to a medieval air. Finally, one reaches a more complete arch, festooned with the Kennedy family's coat of arms, but still not exactly polished. The local sandstone has weathered over time, as Adam surely knew it would.[160] And then there is the house, perched on the edge of the Ayrshire cliffs, looking as if it is about to topple into the sea. The entire approach has built to this, and the house does not disappoint; it is the culmination of the irregular walk, maintaining many of the features of the viaduct—the bartizans, the machicolations, the arrowslits—but standing apart. While the viaduct is an impressive structure in its own right, it merely serves the house, offering previews and underscoring the greater architectural scheme, just as Adam intended.

There is no regularity to the viaduct, nor is there meant to be. The goal is to give an impression, to create an atmosphere, and the viaduct and arch are essential parts of that atmosphere. If the castle stood with a

Opposite: A deliberate suggestion of antiquity. Above right: A favorite motif of Adam's castle style, and one that refers back to the viaduct, these arrowslits on the house complement the bartizans of the viaduct. The Kennedy family coat of arms sits atop an arch more complete than the ruined one at the entrance to the viaduct.

A lesser architect would have been merely pleased with superficial effects to create the castle atmosphere

conventional approach, one regular and straight, what sort of castle would it be? Here Adam's idiosyncratic ideas of architecture flower. When he declared in the preface to the *Works* that "the great masters of antiquity were not so rigidly scrupulous, they varied the proportions as the general spirit of their composition required, clearly perceiving, that however necessary these rules may be to form the taste and to correct the licentiousness of the scholar, they often cramp the genius and circumscribe the ideas of the master," it was no empty boast.[161] As opposed to the rigid Palladians of a generation prior, obsessed with correctness and chastity, Adam sought to create a holistic architecture in which all parts performed at the service of the whole. This he achieved at Culzean, and his commitment to totality in architecture is further borne out by a survey of the viaduct at ground level. A lesser architect would have been merely pleased with superficial effects to create the castle atmosphere; Adam, however, devised a scheme that reinforces impressions at every turn. Passing underneath the viaduct is another roadway, which runs perpendicular to the first stretch of the viaduct proper. Two arches of differing heights further the irregularity of the design, while internal rooms, including an icehouse, accessed via low doorways and giving way to pointed-arch windows, show the viaduct to be much more than a decorative element. The viaduct at Culzean is a virtuoso performance, with every element working in concert to reinforce a singular impression.

OPPOSITE: Passing underneath the viaduct is another roadway, which runs perpendicular to the first stretch of the viaduct proper, emphasizing the asymmetry of the composition.
RIGHT: Nature takes its course, as Adam knew it would.

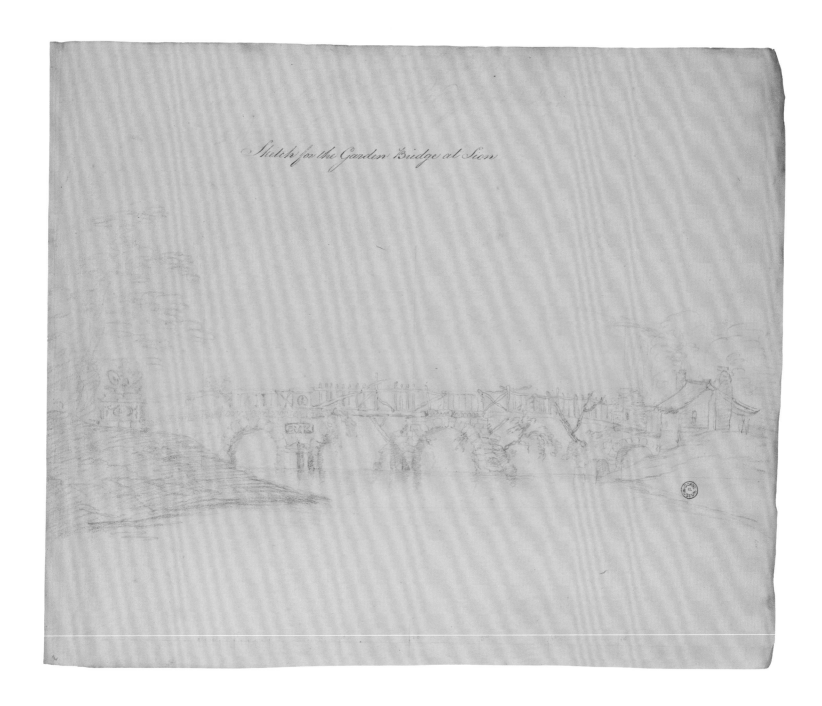

Sketch for the Garden Bridge at Sion

Syon: An Unbuilt Vision

The viaduct at Culzean shows Adam at his most imaginative, finding a creative solution to the problem of uneven land. An examination of some designs Adam prepared for construction, which for various reasons were never erected, will further elucidate Adam's notions of bridge design. These notable bridge schemes—a fantastical garden bridge at Syon and a viaduct at the nexus of Edinburgh's Old and New Towns—though differing in ambition, display the same awareness of composition as his built designs.

Adam reveals thoroughly his conception of bridges in what might be his most farfetched prepared design, for a classical bridge at Syon. He included the bridge in the first volume of the *Works in Architecture of Robert and James Adam* (1773) as part of the suite of illustrations of the ongoing work at Syon House for the Duke and Duchess of Northumberland.

Essentially a promotional exercise, the *Works* was meant to establish firmly the Adam brothers as competent designers of exteriors and interiors to the great and good, while simultaneously showing the primacy of their personal taste in architecture.[162] Eight plates from Syon were included in the first volume, two of which relate to the bridge in question, one including a plan and elevation and the other a perspective view. That Adam should have devoted two of the eight Syon plates to the bridge shows not only his pride in the design but also his certainty, or at least strong hope, that the bridge would be constructed, which, in the end, it almost certainly was not.[163] What is important is that Adam *thought* the bridge would be built, and prepared drawings for it as such.[164] The bridge is a delicate span of three segmental arches, the thin piers bearing carved caryatids, connected by festoons in the spandrels, which enclose carved paterae in the negative space. The balustraded parapet, which contains a central panel populated by arabesques in relief, follows the typical "Aberfeldy profile," with a shallow sweep from the center of the parapets to the edges, terminating in carved sphinxes. Further complicating the design is a course of fluted bands elegantly mimicking voussoirs, and, seen underneath the water in the elevation, barely stepped offsets

Adam reveals thoroughly his conception of bridges in what might be his most farfetched prepared design, for a classical bridge at Syon

OPPOSITE: Robert Adam, *Preliminary Design for a Ruinous Bridge* (Syon House), *ca.* 1763–65, unexecuted. LEFT: Edward Rooker, *Perspective View of the Bridge at Sion*, 1768; This engraving mirrors that contained within the first volume of the *Works in Architecture*.

culminating in curved cutwaters. That Adam went so far as to include detailed illustrations of the depth and position of the piers under the waterline shows his engagement with the practical engineering aspects of the bridge and the degree to which he either thought or hoped the bridge would be built.[165] Thus the bridge displays an extreme tension—one not unknown in other Adam works—between exuberance in design and practicability in construction. No mere flight of fancy, it seems the Syon bridge was intended to be built as drawn, which yields further insight into Adam's design process. While a farfetched design like the Italianate bridge of the previously discussed picturesque watercolor could be used to settle issues in Adam's mind or serve as inspiration for more practicable projects, the overly stylized nature of a presumed-to-be-built design like the Syon bridge is extraordinary. Its appliquéd elements, whereby the ornaments bear only the faintest relation to their utilitarian purposes, contrast with Adam's other bridges and directly rebut Mylne's theories of ornament in the service of utility.

Adam's own words in describing the bridge corroborate how he conceived of such an excessive design. In his description of the bridge in the *Works*, Adam says he "endeavoured to make the decoration light, gay, and graceful, the ideas which naturally arise in beholding the adjacent scenes. The whole is new, and is reckoned fanciful and picturesque ... To suit a building to a scene, requires not only taste but judgment in an artist."[166] This is the closest thing to a credo of bridge design that Adam ever provided. In relating the ornament to those "ideas which naturally arise in beholding the adjacent scenes," he confirmed, at least for his readers' benefit, that his bridges were meant to sit within every project's appropriate stylistic setting: it is why at Audley End a Jacobean-ornamented bridge matching the house gave way to a Palladian bridge; why at Alnwick

RIGHT: "The whole is new, and is reckoned fanciful and picturesque ... To suit a building to a scene, requires not only taste but judgment in an artist." This drawing dates from 1763–65. The nearly identical version in the *Works* includes practical engineering details.

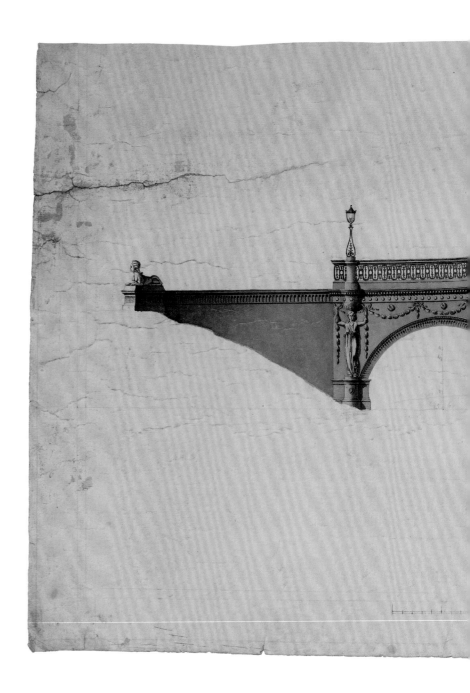

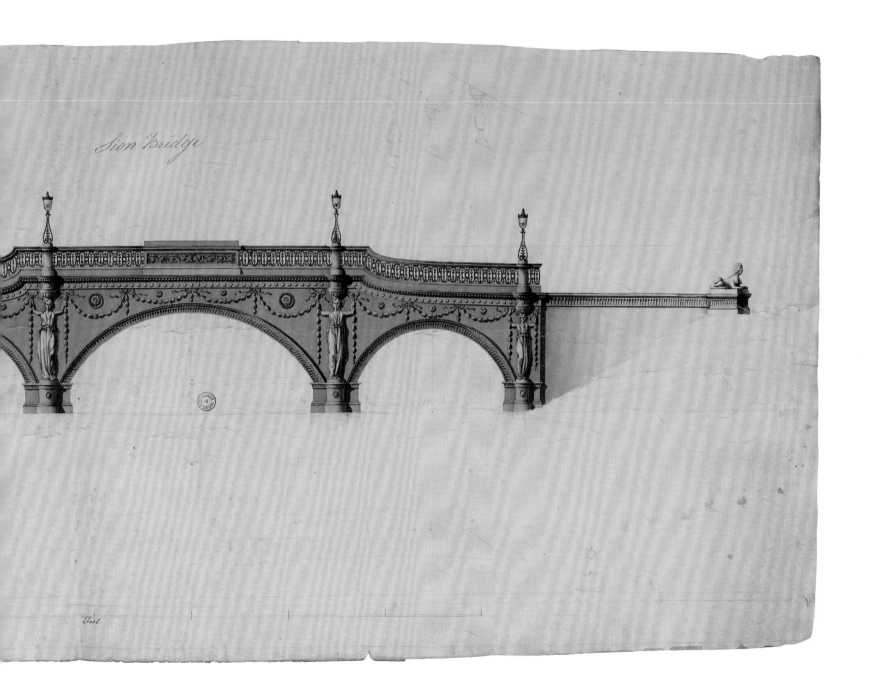

Sion Bridge

Feet

the Lion Bridge was made in a castle style; and why in pointedly neoclassical Bath the Pulteney Bridge's central pediment and Venetian window were deemed fitting. The ornamentation of the bridge at Syon might have been excessive, but it was in keeping with the setting; the Duke of Northumberland had "expressed his desire, that the whole [of Syon] might be executed intirely [sic] in the antique style."[167]

The bridge's markedly antique dressings were also appropriate for a structure intended to make "part of the way leading from the great gate [also designed by Adam] to the house."[168] The gate was to be part of a directed procession, through and over Adam's novel designs to the house, whose interior he so radically remodeled. Adam clearly thought in terms of this procession, which is mirrored by the ordering of the plates for Syon in the *Works*: first the gate, then the bridge, then the house's ground-floor interior.[169] The bridge was merely one—albeit lavishly appointed—stop on Adam's route of genius, as the entrance viaduct to Culzean was. What at first seems to be a curious showpiece is revealed to be an integral part of Adam's architectural composition for Syon.

Not everyone was so keen on the design of the Syon bridge. Horace Walpole had in 1764 praised the Adam redecorations at Syon, writing to the Earl of Hertford that he had "been this evening to Sion, which is becoming another Mount Palatine. Adam has displayed great taste, and the Earl matches it with magnificence."[170] Walpole was so impressed that he hired Adam to work on Strawberry Hill.[171] Even as late as June 1773, Walpole was impressed with Adam's style at Osterley, writing to the Countess of Upper Ossory that,

> On Friday we went to see—oh! the palace of
> palaces!—and yet a palace sans crown, sans coronet,
> but such expense! such taste! such profusion! and yet
> half an acre produces all the rents that furnish such
> magnificence ... The old house I have often seen,
> which was built by Sir Thomas Gresham; but it is so
> improved and enriched, that all the Percies and
> Seymours of Sion must die of envy. There is a double
> portico that fills the space between the towers of the
> front, and is as noble as the Propyleum of Athens.
> There is a hall, library, breakfast-room, eating room,
> all chef d'oeuvres of Adam, a gallery 130 feet long,
> and a drawing room worthy of Eve before the fall ...
> [with] doorcases, and a crimson and gold frieze, that
> I believe were borrowed from the Palace of the Sun.[172]

Months later, however, Walpole had soured upon the Adams' self-congratulatory publication of *The Works in Architecture*: "Mr Adam has published the first number of his 'Architecture.' In it is a magnificent gateway and screen for the Duke of Northumberland at Sion ... all lace and embroidery, and is as 'croquant' as his frames for tables; consequently most improper to be exposed in the high road to Brentford. From Kent's mahogany we are dwindled to Adam's filigree." He goes on to dismiss the Adelphi buildings, the monumental terraces on the Thames that the Adams were then building, as "warehouses laced down the seams, like a soldier's trull [strumpet] in a regimental old coat."[173] The recipient of these letters, the Reverend William Mason, replied on September 12, 1773, that he himself had just seen the Adam brothers' new publication and was not best pleased: "I have just seen the Adams' first number of 'Architecture' and read their preface. Was there ever such a brace of self-puffing Scotch cox-combs? they almost deserve an Heroic Epistle." Working himself up into a frenzy, Walpole piled on five days later, citing the Syon bridge as his breaking point:

> I give up ... any thought that implies an opinion of real curiosity or taste in the present age. The nymphs holding necklaces on the outside of a bridge for Sion in Adams's first number, is a specimen of our productions in architecture, as the preface is of modesty and diffidence.[174]

What Walpole objected to was what he later called Adam's "gingerbread and sippets of embroidery," which is to say the exceedingly stylized and decorative nature of the Syon bridge.[175] And indeed, as a bridge the design must be considered overelaborate, breaking one of the primary rules of bridge building, which is to spend no more time than necessary on ornament, ornament being somewhat ill-at-ease in a functional structure. But Adam had a different approach in mind, wanting instead to play off the adjacent scene, which is to say his new work at Syon House, including the "croquant" entry screen Walpole had also objected to. So went the screen, so went the bridge.

Edinburgh: An Unbuilt Vision

Straddling the line between an intended project and picturesque fantasy are Adam's little-known drawings for a viaduct or "bridge of communication" in Edinburgh linking Princes Street with Calton Hill.[176] It is unclear how seriously Adam approached his various plans for this "bridge of

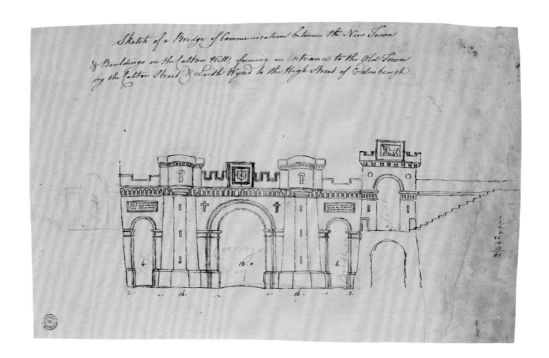

communication." That multiple drawings exist suggests that the idea was more than a lark; that the plans brokered no contemporary comment suggests they may have been private exercises more akin to his picturesque sketches than actual plans meant for consideration by Edinburgh's sundry improvement commissioners.

An examination of the designs for the Calton Hill viaduct again supports the present study's major arguments: that Adam's bridges—always part of some "improving" project—were site-specific and aesthetically contextualized, devised to agree with their surroundings, serving as part of a larger architectural composition. There are two versions of Adam's Calton Hill bridge designs: one more classical in style and the other in the Adam "castle style."[177] For the former, only one drawing survives; of the latter there are four, finished to varying degrees. All the drawings date to around 1791 and are in the Soane Museum. Both versions represent energetic attempts to solve a problem facing Edinburgh at the period: how to connect Calton Hill to both the recently built New Town and the Old Town, the latter then beginning a process of renovation and refurbishment with Adam's Old College (original design 1789) anchoring the plans. Calton Hill was an important site, sitting not only at the eastern reaches of the Royalty of Edinburgh but also directly between the New and Old Towns and abutting the Palace of Holyroodhouse, the royal family's local seat. Until the 1780s the site was mostly undeveloped, housing the old burial

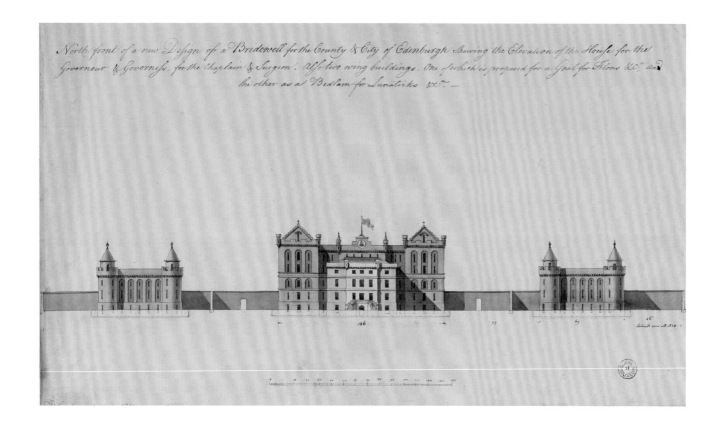

South front towards the Cannongate of the New Bridewell proposed to be built upon the Calton Hill at Edinburgh.

Calton Hill was an important site, sitting not only at the eastern reaches of the
Royalty of Edinburgh but also directly between the New and Old Towns and
abutting the Palace of Holyroodhouse, the royal family's local seat

Opposite: The castle or court revival prototype Bridewell.
Above: The classical prototype Bridewell.

ground (with Adam's classical Mausoleum for David Hume of 1777) and the Old Observatory, designed by James Craig (begun 1769) in a castle style.[178] By the 1780s, the Town Council, which had been so active in directing the construction of the New Town along with its North and South Bridge conveyances, recognized the potential of the Calton Hill site. In 1790, an Act was passed with provisions for the construction of a new Bridewell (reforming prison) and gaol on the Hill.[179]

During the 1780s Robert Adam had quit London to return to Scotland, where he worked on designs for many public schemes and private houses, both in Edinburgh and the surrounding countryside.[180] While most of these public proposals were executed by others, Adam was selected as the architect for the Bridewell; it is in this context that his Calton Hill viaduct designs must be seen. As with the two versions of the Calton Hill bridge, Adam conceived the Bridewell as either a classical or a castle-style building; and, like the bridge designs, the Bridewell drawings all date from near 1791. That Adam thought of the Calton bridge and the Bridewell as linked projects is evidenced by his inclusion of a sketch of the Bridewell in his classical version of the bridge. Seen in the top-left distance behind the bridge, the sketch of the Bridewell corresponds roughly with the more fully worked-up drawing, with a low-slung façade punctuated by low lodges at each end.[181] It is fitting then, that the bridge designed to correspond with this classical prison would present a similarly classical façade. The classical version of the Calton bridge shown in the drawing is an unabashed return to the triumphal type, which had so animated Adam in his earliest bridge designs. Crossing the ravine, the bridge includes a central five-story arch, four pedimented lodges, porticoes, and a course of blind arcades. It is a version of Adam's Pulteney Bridge, but multiplied, vigorously sturdy and relatively unornamented save for engaged columns. It is difficult to believe that Adam thought such a bridge could be built, but it is nonetheless a fascinating object when considered for the way it illustrates his thinking, whereby a bridge forms part of a larger architectural program. While triumphal, the bridge is not an isolated monument, instead relating closely and deliberately to its surroundings. Edinburgh's New Town had been built in a classical style, and Adam was simultaneously designing Charlotte Square, with classical allusions prominently displayed on its façade: festoons, anthemion molding, giant-order Corinthian columns, and more.

The other bridge design, the castle model, sits at the opposite end of Adam's stylistic spectrum.[182] With two machicolated towers for piers, topped by bartizans, the viaduct takes the battlemented ideas explored in Culzean's and goes one step further, incorporating the features Adam had imagined in his picturesque drawing of the Italianate bridge. Beyond this, he crenellates the parapet, providing a castle-style alternative to his usual balustrade. The degree to which this castle-prototype bridge accords with the castle version of the Bridewell that was ultimately built suggests forcefully that Adam considered the prototypes as two separate—indeed dueling—schemes, to be executed in concert one way or the other. The Bridewell as built contained the same harshly angular crenellation, bartizans, and machicolations as the unbuilt viaduct: Ranald MacInnes refers to it as the "Court Revival style."[183] Although the style of this scheme would not match the other Adam designs being executed across town at Charlotte Square, it would agree with James Craig's observatory already standing on Calton Hill and the nearby Palace of Holyroodhouse. What is apparent is that Adam's proposed work on the unbuilt Calton Hill viaduct was not executed in a vacuum. He considered the bridge a part of his greater scheme for Edinburgh, of which the Bridewell was the

OPPOSITE: Edinburgh a decade before Adam's Bridewell design. Thomas Hearne, *Edinburgh, ca.* 1778.

major element in this specific area.[184] That he should attempt to match the style of the bridge to that of the prison is more proof that his bridge designs were always intended to accord with the existing framework of the built environment in a drive for "stylistic as well as logistic cohesion" that was "of the greatest importance in his town planning schemes."[185] Moreover, the inscription on the drawing gives a stronger clue to its stylistic function; not only was it a "bridge of communication between the New Town and Calton Hill," but it also "form[ed] an entrance to the Old Town." The medievalizing style of the proposed castle bridge would have concurred with both the buildings on Calton Hill and the existing architecture in the Old Town. Adam understood the potential of the bridge to serve as a reference for what was to come. He exploited the fact that the bridge has two routes of communication imbued in its structure, with the span leading to Calton Hill and the central arch underneath

leading to the Old Town. He considered how the bridge would be used and designed it to make the most of its setting.

Robert Adam's scenographic conceptualization of bridges contrasted with his peers, who sought to impose designs upon their settings. His drive for aesthetic concord treated bridges as contingent objects, rather than singular monuments to an architect's individual achievement. In this he stands outside most eighteenth-century bridge builders. Bridges changed immensely with the advent of cast iron at the end of the eighteenth century, losing forever their antique ornaments. But for a brief preceding moment, bridges were structures on which to hang monumental classical decoration. Robert Adam, while engaging in some of the typical practices of later eighteenth-century bridge building, prized a different criterion: cohesion. His bridges attempted to fit within their contexts, displaying his facility for broad, scenographic thinking.

ABOVE: The Calton bridge of communication
with classical-style Bridewell at top left.

Dalkeith Palace

On March 10, 1792, seven days after his death from a stomach complaint, Robert Adam was interred at Westminster Abbey. Adam's early pursuit of the great and good came to fruition on his final journey. Among the pallbearers, all titled men save for his former patron William Johnstone Pulteney, who had yet to succeed to his baronetcy, was the Duke of Buccleuch.[186] Just how well Adam knew the Duke is uncertain; he was not one of his major patrons, only contracting for the so-called Montagu Bridge.[187] And though Adam didn't work for Buccleuch until nearly the end of his life, this commission, completed after Adam's death, represented a return to his beginnings.

In 1740, William Adam had, just a few years before his death, designed outbuildings and the so-called Laundry Bridge at Dalkeith for the pallbearing Duke of Buccleuch's grandfather, the second Duke.[188] Life, when examined in hindsight, presents symmetries that are impossible to detect by the living. How charming to see that William Adam, the wellspring of Robert's architectural talent, the man who put him on his way to greatness, had worked for a previous generation of Buccleuchs—generations of respective family businesses, as it were: architects and landowning aristocrats.

And a comparison of William's 1740 Laundry Bridge with the Montagu Bridge of 1792 reveals just how far Robert Adam had moved beyond his father's model. The Laundry Bridge is a solid, everyday thing: three piers, two elliptical arches, the only ornament a dropped keystone projecting atop the central voussoir of each arch. Each pier bumps out slightly, a vestigial nod to fortification, but the whole affair is low-lying and reticent, as befits its neighborhood: it gets its name from the laundry house, also to William Adam's design, nearby. If the Laundry Bridge is a shrub, Adam's Montagu Bridge is a noble, mighty oak—rising majestically, more related to the sky than the ground.

The unabashed grandeur of the Montagu Bridge reflects its origins as a celebratory work. In 1790, the third Duke's wife, Elizabeth (née Montagu), by virtue of her family's male line dying out, secured the Montagu titles and estates for her own children.[189] Such a consolidation could not go without celebration, and the result is a fittingly grand structure. The arch's seventy-foot span and forty-two-foot height are imposing, made even more so by the fact that it is a single arch; whereas Adam's other bridges tend to distribute weight across multiple arches, orienting the works horizontally, the Montagu

OPPOSITE: A single arch with a seventy-foot span and forty-two foot height: imposing, and thrusting upwards.

Bridge thrusts upwards, its structural walls disappearing into the hills, leaving just the arch itself as the focus.[190] The decorative elements are spare, and have only become more so over time. Adam's initial drawing for the scheme confirms the basic form of the bridge as it was built but dresses it up. A Buccleuch stag trippant stands atop the central pedestal (where is his wife's heraldry, one dares to ask) while niches on the piers contain urns, these columned in the Doric order with pediments atop. The final design lost its tabernacles, and the rectangular panels their scrollwork. Gone too, are the reclining sculptures above the piers, seemingly copied directly from Adam's single-arch design for the bridge at Kedleston years prior. Maintained, however, is the carved frieze, simple circles in squares, lending the bridge an air of quiet dignity. The stag died not as a result of the architect's usual paring-down process, but because it was scaring horses on this most essential approach and was therefore taken down.[191]

OPPOSITE: Adam's original design for the Montagu Bridge at
Dalkeith was a rather busier affair than the executed bridge.
ABOVE: The final design pared down the exuberance of the initial
effort, losing the tabernacles and reclining sculptures.

It's fortunate that the bridge, as built, lacks the ornament of the initial drawing, for such decoration could only distract from what is a magnificent structure *qua* structure. Intended, as the drawing's inscription says, "to pass in the new approach from Edinburgh to Dalkeith House," the bridge's fundamental purpose is in relation to the house. Grand and large as the bridge is, its job is conveyance—the house is the goal. And that goal is in full view as one crosses the bridge, with the structure's low parapet giving unrestricted visual access to the house. Even more, if one stands on the riverbank just north of the bridge, the massive arch frames the house, containing the historical structure within the new one. The picturesque logic was understood by Adam and by later visitors. Consider an 1819 watercolor by George Heriot, now in the collection of the Yale Center for British Art.[192] Though the bridge and house are embowered, both are present in the scene, being explicitly part of the same composition. The bridge gives foreground to the house, and the jutting wing of the main structure sits directly behind the bridge, inexorably tying the two together. And though the house predates the bridge by almost a century (it was substantially rebuilt starting around 1702), the bridge is a deliberate partner in the house's glory.[193] The bridge is on a private estate, but it is not exactly an estate bridge, no mere private road. It links country to town in heroic fashion, serving as the principal approach to the ducal abode from the capital city, altogether appropriate to the family's status and the house to which it is attached. Adam applied the lessons of a lifetime at Dalkeith, and we can consider ourselves fortunate that this bridge, like many others, is still accessible today.

The bridge gives foreground to the house, and the jutting wing of the main structure sits directly behind the bridge, inexorably tying the two together

ABOVE: Later viewers understood the logic. George Heriot, *View of a Bridge*, 1819. OPPOSITE: The bridge and the house: deliberate partners in glory.

Glossary

Abutment
The support structure at the end of a bridge.

Aedicule
A frame on a wall consisting of two columns and an entablature, usually topped by a pediment. A **tabernacle** is a simple aedicule.

Anthemion
From the Greek for flower-like, a decorative ornament approximating floral forms.

Arabesque
A nonfigurative surface decoration involving the interlacing of lines.

Arch ring ①
The face of the arch that shows outwards in elevation.

Arch
A curved structure spanning an open space and supporting what lies above it. Arches may be **semicircular**, having a rise equal to half its span; **elliptical** ②, flatter, with a rise less than half its span; **segmental**, also with a rise less than half its span but generally taller than elliptical arches; **pointed**, with a rise greater than half its span.
A **blind arch** is one applied merely to the surface of a wall. A **relieving arch** is incorporated into a wall above the arch opening itself.

Archivolt ③
A molding atop the arch ring that projects.

Arrowslit
A narrow opening in a wall from which to launch arrows. The space behind an arrowslit is an **embrasure**.

Baluster ④
From the Greek for pomegranate flower, a pillar supporting a rail with a bulbous shape. A series of balusters forms a **balustrade** ⑤.

Column
An upright supporting structure featuring a base, shaft, and capital. Multiple columns in a row form a **colonnade**, the space behind which is a **loggia**. A **caryatid** is a sculptural depiction of a female figure upholding an entablature, thereby taking the place of a column.

Entablature
Collectively, the three parts of a classical building that sit above a column. The entablature is composed of an **architrave**, or lintel, the piece sitting directly atop the columns; the **frieze**, the middle band of ornament (or more generally any band of ornament); the **cornice**, the top projecting ledge. A **dentil cornice**, from the Latin for tooth, has projecting rectangular blocks resembling their namesake.

Festoon

A carved ornament resembling a garland, usually of fruit or flowers, hung up at two ends. Also called a **swag** when depicting fabric.

Finial

The topmost ornamental feature of any structure.

Masonry

Any stonework.

Obelisk

An upright, square pillar terminating in a pyramid shape.

Parapet

A wall that protects from any large drop on the other side. A **battlement** is a fortified parapet with alternating spaces (**embrasures**) and pieces that project upwards (**merlons**). Battlement is also known as **crenellation**. Underneath battlements are often found **machicolations**, openings originally for the dropping of missiles.

Pediment ⑥

A triangular gable atop columns.

Pier ⑦

The vertical support structure between two arches. A **cutwater** ⑧ is the bottom of a pier that juts out at an angle to redirect the stream.

Portico

A covered porch with columns supporting it, usually at the entrance to a structure.

Quoin

Stones at the angle of a structure that project to create contrast.

Roundel

A circular ornament. If carved like a dish, it is called a **patera**.

Rustication

Any method of using masonry to convey an impression of rough robustness, usually in contrast to adjacent smooth stone.

Scroll

Spiral-based ornament.

Spandrel ⑨

The space on top of the arch ring and below the deck of a bridge.

Trippant

In heraldry, a stag moving towards the left of the viewer, with its right front hoof raised and all others on the ground.

Turret

A tiny tower, usually attached to a greater structure. A **bartizan** is a turret that projects over a wall.

Venetian Window ⑩

A window consisting of a central arched light, with two rectangular sidelights flanking and each sidelight framed by twinned columns or pilasters. Also called a **Serliana** or **Palladian** window.

Viaduct

A structure like a bridge, but crossing low ground rather than water.

Voussoir ⑪

A wedge-shaped stone composing the arch. The centermost voussoir is called a **keystone**.

Wing wall

A side wall extending out to support further the abutment of a bridge

Endnotes

Preface

1 A. A. Tait, *Robert Adam: Drawings and Imagination*, Cambridge Studies in the History of Architecture (Cambridge: Cambridge University Press, 1993): 85.

2 As Tait says, "The rapid expansion of the office after the return of James and his band of *émigré* artists in 1763, meant that the tying of a hand to a particular name became almost impossible. The thoroughly professional drawings by [Agostino] Brunias for stucco and arabesque work at Kedleston of around 1760, were indistinguishable four year later from a group of similarly accomplished but anonymous hands. See: Tait, *Robert Adam: Drawings and Imagination*, 93–94.

3 Sir John Soane's Museum, London, Spiers box-file ("Papers connected with Purchases"), Laing to Soane, December 12, 1832, as quoted in Iain Gordon Brown, "Robert Adam's Drawings: Edinburgh's Loss, London's Gain," in *The Book of the Old Edinburgh Club* New Series 2 (1992): 24.

Chapter I
Beginnings

4 Quoted in John Fleming, *Robert Adam and His Circle: In Edinburgh & Rome* (London: John Murray, 1962): 113.

5 Fleming, *Robert Adam and His Circle*, 115–16.

6 Fleming, *Robert Adam and His Circle*, 116.

7 John Gifford, *William Adam, 1689–1748: The Life and Times of Scotland's Universal Architect* (Edinburgh: Mainstream Publishing, 1989): 68.

8 Gifford, *William Adam*, 71–72.

9 Quoted in Gifford, *William Adam*, 72. Gifford suggests Adam had left school by 1704.

10 Quoted in John Gifford, "William Adam and the Historians," *Architectural Heritage* I (1990): 1.

11 Quoted in William R. M. Kay, "What's His Line: Would the Real William Adam Please Stand Up? Some Recent Research Discoveries," *Architectural Heritage* I (1990): 50.

12 Gifford, *William Adam*, 74.

13 Gifford, *William Adam*, 86.

14 Gifford, *William Adam*, 79.

15 Quoted in Gifford, *William Adam*, 76.

16 Gifford, *William Adam*, 107–10.

17 Quoted in Gifford, *William Adam*, 183–84.

18 Quoted in Fleming, *Robert Adam and His Circle*, 102.

19 Fleming, *Robert Adam and His Circle*, 6.

20 Quoted in Gifford, *William Adam*, 183.

21 Fleming, *Robert Adam and His Circle*, 79. The Alexander Monro who taught Robert anatomy was the first, known subsequently as "*primus*."

22 Fleming, *Robert Adam and His Circle*, 52.

23 For a full account of William Adam's library, see Alistair Rowan, "William Adam's Library," *Architectural Heritage* I (1990): 8–33.

24 Fleming, *Robert Adam and His Circle*, 80. It was the estate at Dowhill that allowed Robert to sit successfully for a seat in Parliament.

25 Fleming, *Robert Adam and His Circle*, 84.

26 Ted Ruddock, *Arch Bridges and Their Builders, 1735–1835* (Cambridge: Cambridge University Press, 1979): 19.

27 Ruddock, *Arch Bridges*, 19–25.

28 Fleming, *Robert Adam and His Circle*, 85–86.

29 Fleming, *Robert Adam and His Circle*, 92–93.

30 Quoted in Fleming, *Robert Adam and His Circle*, 95.

31 Quoted in Fleming, *Robert Adam and His Circle*, 96.

32 Fleming, *Robert Adam and His Circle*, 95.

33 As Fleming says, it "is as if the patron, in a fit of economy, had stripped his architects' design down to its bare bones." Fleming, *Robert Adam and His Circle*, 95.

34 Robert Adam and James Adam, *The Works in Architecture of Robert and James Adam* (London: Printed for the Authors, 1778). For A. T. Bolton's discussion of the concept of "total effect," see Arthur T. Bolton, *The Architecture and Decoration of Robert Adam and Sir John Soane, R.A. (1758–1837),* (London: Wm. Clowes & Sons, 1920): 12.

35 Simpson & Brown, for the Great Steward of Scotland's Dumfries House Trust, *Draft Conservation Plan: Introduction & Historical Development*, Volume 1 (Edinburgh: Simpson & Brown, 2008): 82.

36 Simpson & Brown, *Draft Conservation Plan*, 85.

37 The current entrance to the house is off the A70, south of the house, but the Temple gateway provided access north from Auchincleck.

38 Adam & Adam, *The Works in Architecture*, I, Preface, 3.

39 Others have attributed the bridge to John, but as it was John and Robert, and not James, who were involved in the building at Inveraray, such speculation may be a mug's game. James was still in school at the time. See: David King, *The Complete Works of Robert and James Adam* (Oxford: The Architectural Press, 2001): 338; Ian G. Lindsay and Mary Cosh, *Inveraray and the Dukes of Argyll* (Edinburgh: Edinburgh University Press, 1973): 136–40, and Fleming, *Robert Adam and His Circle*, 64. The plate in *Vitruvius Scoticus* is number 74.

40 Ruddock, *Arch Bridges*, 118.

41 For a full account of John's involvement, see Simpson & Brown, *Draft Conservation Plan*, 34–63.

42 Simpson & Brown, *Draft Conservation Plan*, 80.

43 John Summerson, *Georgian London*, edited by Howard Colvin (New Haven: Published for the Paul Mellon Centre for Studies in British Art by Yale University Press, 2003): 105.

44 Howard, Colvin, *A Biographical Dictionary of British Architects, 1600–1840, Third Edition* (New Haven and London: Yale University Press, 1995): 52.

45 Quoted in Fleming, *Robert Adam and His Circle*, 279.

46 Robert Adam, *The Works* IV, Public Buildings, Preface.

47 Though the Adelphi was privately funded, the combination of its scale and the concessions needed from public bodies to facilitate its construction place it very much within the realm of a public building project.

Chapter II
Bridges in Eighteenth-Century Britain

48 Samuel Johnson, *The Letters of Samuel Johnson*, Volume I: 1719–1774, Collected & Edited by R. W. Chapman (Oxford: Clarendon Press, 1952): 464. The quotation is found in a December 1, 1759, letter to the London *Daily Gazette* surrounding the Blackfriars Bridge competition. For a full discussion of Johnson's involvement in the Blackfriars debate, see Morris R. Brownell, *Samuel Johnson's Attitude to the Arts* (Oxford: Clarendon Press, 1989): 107–36.

49 The first major work on Adam, and still useful, is Arthur T. Bolton, *The Architecture of Robert & James Adam* (1758–1794) (New York: Scribner, 1922). For broader discussions of Adam's work, David King's catalogue raisonné provides the most complete listing. See: King, *The Complete Works*. For Adam's interiors, see

Eileen Harris, *The Genius of Robert Adam: His Interiors* (New Haven and London: Yale University Press for the Paul Mellon Centre for Studies in British Art, 2001). On Adam's picturesque drawings, see Tait, *Robert Adam: Drawings and Imagination*. The only Adam bridge project to receive sustained scholarly attention is the Pulteney Bridge in Bath. See: Jean Manco, "Pulteney Bridge," *Architectural History* 38 (1995): 129–45.

50 Robert Mylne was, among Adam's contemporaries, the only prolific bridge builder, with eleven bridges either fully or partially designed and built by him. Adam's built designs surpass this in number, if not necessarily ambition. Adam's other rivals were not much concerned with bridges after the Blackfriars competition.

51 Ruddock, *Arch Bridges*, 116. This number includes the so-called "picturesque" drawings.

52 Mark Girouard, *The English Town* (New Haven and London: Yale University Press, 1990): 86. The full list Girouard gives is nearly all-encompassing: "'Improvement' was much in the air in the eighteenth century. Methods of commerce could be improved, by the provision of better quays, docks, and warehouses. Manufacture could be improved, by techniques such as the application of steam power ... transport could be improved, by the formation of canals, the building of bridges and the making of turnpike trusts. Agriculture could be improved, by enclosure and better methods of farming. Towns could be improved, by the paving, lighting, straightening and widening of streets, the formation of new streets, the destruction of medieval town walls, the provision of water, the laying out of public walks, and the erection of public buildings. Country houses could be improved, by being rebuilt or remodeled in a purer taste, or given a new setting of idyllic parkland. The arts could be improved, by enlightened patronage and the founding of academies. The condition of the poor could be improved, by the provision of schools, hospitals and better prisons." For specific reference to garden improvement schemes, see Tom Williamson, *The Transformation of Rural England: Farming and the Landscape 1700–1870* (Exeter: University of Exeter Press, 2002): 79, 19.

53 For a discussion of the rise of the term "improvement" and the fashionability of the idea, see Sarah Tarlow, *The Archaeology of Improvement in Britain, 1750–1850*, Cambridge Studies in Archaeology (Cambridge and New York: Cambridge University Press, 2007): 1–34.

54 There was a bridge at Fulham by 1729, but Fulham was then suburban territory. See Ruddock, *Arch Bridges*, 3.

55 Ruddock, *Arch Bridges*, 3. The presence of so many piers created spans that made it difficult for the water to pass under them without redirection; the low rises of the piers impeded ships with tall masts from passing underneath.

56 Summerson, *Georgian London*, 107.

57 Nicholas Hawksmoor, *A Short Historical Account of London-Bridge, With a Proposition for a New Stone-Bridge at Westminster: As Also an Account of Some Remarkable Stone-Bridges Abroad, and What the Best Authors Have Said and Directed Concerning The Methods of Building Them* (London: J. Wilcox, 1736).

58 Ruddock, *Arch Bridges*, 3.

59 J. Mordaunt Crook, "The Pre-Victorian Architect: Professionalism & Patronage," *Architectural History* 12 (1969): 64. It was perfectly normal for Hawksmoor— who incidentally presented Palladio's rules concerning the proportions of piers and arches as doctrine—to involve himself in Westminster Bridge, especially with his experience in bridge construction at Blenheim (1708–24), just as it was natural that Robert Mylne should build the Blackfriars (1759), or Robert Adam the Pulteney Bridge (1770). For Hawksmoor on Palladio, see Hawksmoor, *A Short Historical Account of London-Bridge*, 24.

60 Ruddock, *Arch Bridges*, 4. Labelye had described himself in 1736 as "Engineer, late teacher of Mathematics in the Royal Navy" on a survey map of the Kentish coast.

61 Summerson, *Georgian London*, 110. The balustraded parapet was, however, the first for a major bridge project. See: Andrew Saint, *Architect and Engineer: A Study in Sibling Rivalry* (New Haven and London: Yale University Press, 2007): 308.

62 Bernard Forest de Bélidor, *Architecture Hydraulique*, Volume IV (Paris, 1752), 192. Quoted in translation in Ruddock, *Arch Bridges*, 18. Summerson asserted that Westminster Bridge was a "standard which was recognized by Gwynn, Mylne and Smeaton, Telford and the Rennies" and the "foundation of an English tradition in bridge building second to none in Europe." See: Summerson, *Georgian London*, 110.

63 Rowan, "William Adam's Library," 13. For a translation of Bélidor's rules for bridges, see Ruddock, *Arch Bridges*, 202.

64 Summerson, *Georgian London*, 120. Summerson counts "the Embankment, Waterloo Bridge, Trafalgar Square, Bedford Square, Finsbury Square, Moorgate

Street, Cranbourn Street, and dozens of minor improvements" among Gwynn's suggestions.

65 Ruddock, *Arch Bridges*, 63. Gwynn did, however, submit a design for the bridge, showing his consistent engagement with the task of London's improvement. The result of a debate about whether to rebuild London Bridge or build a new bridge entirely had resulted in a decision to do both. The City had, evidently, by that time, lost its antipathy towards new bridges.

66 Summerson, *Georgian London*, 121.

67 Damie Stillman, *English Neo-Classical Architecture* (London: Zwemmer, 1988): 94–95.

68 Mylne's grand tour, it must be said, was considerably less lavish than Adam's, something the latter did not fail to mention.

69 Ruddock, *Arch Bridges*, 64.

70 Quoted in Fleming, *Robert Adam and His Circle*, 116. Fleming suggests Adam's skipping of Orange and St. Remy while in Roman France demonstrates "that he was more readily impressed by feats of Roman engineering than by examples of more strictly architectural accomplishment, such as the Maison Carrée at Nîmes, about which he has nothing to say." With its repeated pattern of wide arches and low doors it anticipates the similar motif used in the Culzean viaduct.

71 Westminster is, of course, technically astylar in its lack of classical orders.

72 The exception seems to be John Smeaton's design, which rehashes closely the unelaborate Westminster design but replaces the semicircles with ellipses. Smeaton was, on the architect–engineer continuum much more an engineer. See Ruddock, *Arch Bridges*, 68–69.

73 Ruddock, *Arch Bridges*, 66. For a full description of Chambers's entry, see Stillman, *English Neo-Classical Architecture*: 95.

74 John Bonehill, "'The Centre of Pleasure and Magnificence': Paul and Thomas Sandby's London," *Huntington Library Quarterly* 75, no. 3 (2012): 385.

75 Piranesi was a "warm friend of Mylne, an acquaintance at least of Chambers, and [later] a tutor and friend of the son of George Dance," while also maintaining friendly relations with Robert Adam, to whom he dedicated his book of views of the Campus Martius. Ruddock, *Arch Bridges*, 66. For more on the Piranesi/Adam relationship, see Fleming, *Robert Adam and His Circle*, 165–68; 174; 207–08; 228; 230; 354; 364; 374.

76 Tom Williamson, *Polite Landscapes: Garden and Society in Eighteenth-Century England* (Stroud, Gloucestershire: Allan Sutton, 1995): 61.

77 Ruddock, *Arch Bridges*, 66.

78 Publicus [Robert Mylne], *Observations on Bridge Building, and the Several Plans Offered for a New Bridge* (London: J. Townsend, 1760): 25.

79 Publicus [Robert Mylne], *Observations on Bridge Building*, 24.

80 Publicus [Robert Mylne], *Observations on Bridge Building*, 39.

81 John Smeaton, *Mr. Smeaton's Answer to the Misrepresentations of His Plan for Black-Friars Bridge, Contained in a Late Anonymous Pamphlet, Addressed to the Gentlemen of the Committee for Building a Bridge at Black-Friars* (London, 1760): 2.

82 The presence of the arms of the City of London, coupled with the 1758/1759 date is the clue that these designs were intended for the Blackfriars competition. See: Stillman, *English Neo-Classical Architecture*, 95. The design call numbers in the Soane catalogue are: Soane Museum Adam Volume 9/82; 9/72; 9/73, the first of which gives the most complete view.

83 Quoted in Fleming, *Robert Adam and His Circle*, 211–12.

84 Quoted in Fleming, *Robert Adam and His Circle*, 272.

85 Quoted in Fleming, *Robert Adam and His Circle*, 295–96.

86 Fleming, *Robert Adam and His Circle*, 188. Mylne recognized the gap in means between Adam and him on their respective grand tours, writing to his father that Adam "makes a great figure here by keeping a coach and a couple of footmen ... [but] I assure you, as an architect he makes no more figure than we do ourselves ..."

87 Mylne called Gwynn's entry a "Turkey-carpet," and a "trifling geegaw," which gives a sense of how even contemporary observers saw the design as overwrought. See: Publicus [Robert Mylne], *Observations on Bridge Building*, 22. Quoted in Bonehill, "'The Centre of Pleasure and Magnificence,'" 387.

88 The piers-with-aedicules design recalls Palladio's design for the Rialto Bridge. Chambers's design for Blackfriars also included aedicules.

89 See Stillman, *English Neo-Classical Architecture*, 95, for a full description of the Adam Blackfriars submission. The design eventually built at Kedleston (SM Adam Volume 40/42) pares back the exuberance of the first design, a process endlessly repeated in Adam's bridge-building career.

90 Ruddock, *Arch Bridges*, 18; Bonehill, "'The Centre of Pleasure and Magnificence,'" 385–86.

91 Bonehill, "'The Centre of Pleasure and Magnificence,'" 374.

92 Quoted in Bonehill, "'The Centre of Pleasure and Magnificence,'" 374. Soane also produced a drawing for a bridge of magnificence in 1776, a three-dimensional view of Westminster, that exceeds Sandby's in imagination with the dramatically curved wings of its entrance pavilions. See: Anthony Wylson, *Aquatecture: Architecture and Water* (London: The Architectural Press, 1986): 99.

93 Ranald MacInnes, "Robert Adam's Bridges," in *The Architecture of Scottish Cities: Essays in Honour of David Walker*, edited by Deborah Mays (East Linton: Tuckwell Press, 1997): 78.

94 Adam & Adam, *The Works in Architecture*, 10.

Chapter III
Robert Adam's Estate Bridges

95 King, *The Complete Works*, 31.

96 The foremost fortified structures Adam built are found in Alnwick Castle's "Lion Bridge" and Culzean Castle's entrance viaduct.

97 For more on the bridge at Dumfries House see Simon Green, *Dumfries House: An Architectural Story*, edited by Jane Thomas (Edinburgh: Royal Commission on the Ancient and Historical Monuments of Scotland, 2014): 123–24; Ruddock, *Arch Bridges*, 118; King, *The Complete Works*, 398–99. For the bridges at Inveraray see King, *The Complete Works*, 337–38.

98 The view is now blocked by plantings.

99 Adam also mined this work on a physical level: the so-called "Gothick Bridge" at Inveraray (1759) anticipates Adam's early work at Audley End, with its quatrefoil piercings, and his Lion Bridge at Alnwick with its tower-topped piers and crenellated parapet.

100 Quoted in Colin Thom, "Introduction. 'Some Promising Young Men': Robert Adam and His Brothers," in *Robert Adam and His Brothers: New Light on Britain's Leading Architectural Family*, edited by Colin Thom, (Swindon: Historic England, 2019): 5. There is an exceedingly elaborate covered bridge design for Mitcham Grove in the Soane Museum (9/85), with domed pavilions at either end and a central statue above the colonnade, but this dates to *circa* 1770–73 and was made for Alexander Wedderburn, who had bought Mitcham from the Stewart family.

101 J. D. Williams, *Audley End: The Restoration of 1762–1797*, Essex Record Office ((Chelmsford: Essex County Council (Record Office), 1966)): 4–6. Griffin Griffin had inherited Audley End after earlier agreeing with his aunt to change his surname to Griffin from Whitwell. Adam had by 1762 achieved some success in his newly established London architectural practice, most notably with the remodeling of Kedleston Hall (begun 1760) and interior redecoration of Syon House (begun 1761). He was a natural enough choice for Griffin Griffin's ambitious restoration project at Audley End, where his interior work was a relatively small part of the house's greater improvement plan, totaling just over £190 of labor. The aforementioned projects and the construction of the Admiralty Screen at Whitehall signaled Adam's arrival on the London architectural scene. For Adam's labor bills, see Williams, *Audley End*, 33. Adam added kitchen offices and created and decorated a new suite in the house's south wing. See: King, *Complete Works*, 198.

102 Williams, *Audley End*, 19.

103 Williams, *Audley End*, 19.

104 Williams, *Audley End*, 44.

105 Williams, *Audley End*, 45–46.

106 Williams, *Audley End*, 46. Saffron Walden is the closest town to Audley End. An 1845 account notes that the bridge was constructed "for the use of the publick."

107 King, *Complete Works*, 323.

108 Ruddock, *Arch Bridges*, 118.

109 Nikolaus Pevsner and James Bettley, *Essex*, Pevsner Architectural Guides (New Haven and London: Yale University Press, 2007): 104. Pevsner claims the design as built takes inspiration from Palladio's bridge over the Bacchiglione in Vicenza, but the design is similar to the bridge at Dumfries House, too; it is safe to say Adam drew on a variety of sources.

110 Tim Mowl, *Palladian Bridges: Prior Park and the Whig Connection* (Bath: Millstream Books in association with the Bath Preservation Trust, 1993): 9. Pembroke had served, essentially, as the patron of the Westminster Bridge project, and his familiarity with bridge design and construction allowed him to adapt a convincingly Palladian idiom for his own Wilton project. See: Ruddock, *Arch Bridges*, 11.

111 Mowl, *Palladian Bridges*, 34–37. The Palladian bridge was so fashionable it later appeared at Tsarskoe Selo, Catherine the Great's summer residence.

112 The mason for the tea-house bridge was John Devall (junior), the son of the mason John Devall who had constructed the bridge at Wilton. See: Mowl, *Palladian Bridges*, 9 and Williams, *Audley End*, 47.

113 Quoted in Fleming, *Robert Adam and His Circle*, 218. His Pulteney Bridge also pares back Palladio, in that case the unbuilt design for the Rialto Bridge, Venice.

114 For a full account of Alnwick, see Colin Shrimpton, *Alnwick Castle: Home of the Duke of Northumberland* (Derby: Heritage House Group, 2004).

115 King, *Complete Works*, 242–44. For a full account of the Duchess's gothic leanings, see Laura Mayer, "Landscape as Legacy: Elizabeth Percy, 1st Duchess of Northumberland, and the Gothick Garden Buildings of Alnwick, Northumberland," *Garden History* 39, no. 1 (2011): 34–50. The exuberantly neoclassical interior redecoration at Syon undertaken by Adam is likely to have been at the behest of the Duke.

116 It is worth remembering that Elizabeth Seymour, the Duchess of Northumberland, was the Percy in the family. The Duke, originally Sir Hugh Smithson, took the Percy name upon marriage to Elizabeth in 1740. See: Mayer, "Landscape as Legacy," 34.

117 Mayer, "Landscape as Legacy," 35.

118 Mayer, "Landscape as Legacy," 37.

119 Mayer, "Landscape as Legacy," 35.

120 His outrageous design for a classical bridge at Syon with caryatids was never built despite being illustrated in *The Works*. See chapter V for a fuller discussion.

121 David McFetrich, *An Encyclopaedia of British Bridges* (Yorkshire: Pen and Sword Transport, 2019): 184.

122 Oliver Wendell Holmes was never able to forget the Percy lion's straight-out tail, relating in *The Autocrat of the Breakfast-Table*, "I remember the Percy lion on the bridge over the little river at Alnwick, the leaden lion with his tail stretched out straight like a pump-handle,—and why? Because of the story of the village boy who must fain bestride the leaden tail, standing out over the water,—which breaking, he dropped into the stream far below, and was taken out an idiot for the rest of his life." See: Oliver Wendell Holmes, *The Autocrat of the Breakfast-Table: Every Man His Own Boswell* (Boston: Houghton, Mifflin and Company, 1895): 281.

123 J. Mordaunt Crook, "Northumbrian Gothick," *Journal of the Royal Society of Arts* 121, no. 5201 (1973): 279.

124 Mayer, "Landscape as Legacy," 39.

125 The painting is now in the collection of the Art Gallery of South Australia, accession number 0.1814.

126 Turner first sketched Alnwick in 1799, only returning to the composition three decades later. The Tate, which owns the original sketch, suggests that the lack of prominence and detail given to the decorative lion on the bridge owes to the fact that Turner sketched the bridge at night and thus could not make out the particulars in the dim light. See: Andrew Wilton, "*Alnwick Castle, with the Lion Bridge* 1797 by Joseph Mallord William Turner," catalogue entry, January 2013, in David Blayney Brown, editor, *J. M. W. Turner: Sketchbooks, Drawings and Watercolours* (London: Tate Research Publication, November 2014).

127 As Martin Sonnabend contended, "it is no exaggeration to say that nearly all [Claude's] paintings, drawings, and—to a lesser extent—prints have been in British collections at one time or another." See: Martin Sonnabend, "Claude Lorrain: The Enchanted Landscape," in *Claude Lorrain: The Enchanted Landscape*, by Martin Sonnabend and Jon Whitely, with Christian Rümelin (Oxford: Ashmolean Museum, in association with Lund Humphries): 17.

128 Tait, *Robert Adam: Drawings and Imagination*, 10–11.

129 The painting had entered England by 1753, but even if Adam was unaware of this exact picture, he was certainly aware of the type. See: Martin Sonnabend and Jon Whitely, with Christian Rümelin, *Claude Lorrain: The Enchanted Landscape*, 36. The painting is now at the Birmingham Museum & Art Gallery, accession number 1955P111.

Chapter IV
The Pulteney Bridge, Bath

130 The Corporation was the governing body of the city.

131 John Wood, *A Description of Bath*, (London: W. Bathoe and T. Lownds, 1765): 224. The 1765 edition quoted here is a corrected posthumous edition; Wood died in 1754.

132 Walter Ison, *The Georgian Buildings of Bath*, 1700–1830 (Bath: Kingsmead, 1980): 5.

133 Wood, *A Description of Bath*, 225.

134 Ison, *The Georgian Buildings of Bath*, 6. Wood had returned to Bath from Yorkshire and London by 1727.

135 Wood, *A Description of Bath*, 341.

136 Ison, *The Georgian Buildings of Bath*, 7. Added to Bath's architectural patrimony were Wood the Younger's Assembly Rooms (1769–71), with exteriors unremarkable save for the way they corresponded with the existing houses radiating out from the Circus. Adam himself had produced designs for the Assembly Rooms in the years *circa* 1765–68, but his plans were thought too expensive and Wood the Younger's were chosen instead. For Adam's elevation, see Soane Museum Adam Volume 28/45; for the plans, see SM Adam Volume 28/49; for an axial section, see SM Adam Volume 28/47.

137 Peter Borsay, *The Image of Georgian Bath, 1700–2000* (Oxford: Oxford University Press, 2000): 144.

138 *The Bath and Bristol Guide, or Tradesman's and Traveller's Pocket-Companion* (Bath: Thomas Boddely, 1753): 4. The 1755 edition is quoted in Borsay, *The Image of Georgian Bath*, 25.

139 Borsay, *The Image of Georgian Bath*, 147.

140 R. S. Neale, *Bath 1680–1850: A Social History or A Valley of Pleasure, Yet a Sink of Iniquity* (London: Routledge & Kegan Paul, 1981): 226–27.

141 Letter from William Johnstone Pulteney to Lord Darlington, August 23, 1769, quoted in Jean Manco, "Pulteney Bridge," 130.

142 Neale, *Bath 1680–1850*, 228. The original source is in the Pulteney Estate Papers, Manuscript 1809, Bundle 6.

143 Neale, *Bath 1680–1850*, 231.

144 The surviving evidence for the Adam's Bathwick scheme exists only in drawings at the Soane Museum.

145 Neale, *Bath 1680–1850*, 231. The original source is in the Pulteney Estate Papers, Manuscript 1809, Bundle 6.

146 A copy of Leoni's translation of Palladio was in the library at Blair Adam. See: Rowan, "William Adam's Library," 28.

147 Ison, *The Georgian Buildings of Bath*, 47.

148 Undated letter from Mayor, Alderman, and Common Council of Bath to William Johnstone Pulteney, quoted in Neale, *Bath 1680–1850*, 233. Original in Huntington Library, California, PU 57.

149 Undated letter from Mayor, Alderman, and Common Council of Bath to William Johnstone Pulteney, quoted in Neale, *Bath 1680–1850*, 233. Original in Huntington Library, California, PU 57.

150 Alistair Rowan, *Vaulting Ambition: The Adam Brothers:*

Contractors to the Metropolis in the Reign of George III. London: Sir John Soane's Museum, 2007: 68–69.

151 David Watkin editor, *Sir John Soane: Enlightenment Thought and the Royal Academy Lectures* (Cambridge: Cambridge University Press, 1996): 393.

152 J. Earle, *A Guide to the Knowledge of Bath Ancient and Modern* (London, 1864): 124, quoted in Borsay, *The Image of Georgian Bath*, 203.

153 *The Original Bath Guide* (Bath, 1876): 115, quoted in Borsay, *The Image of Georgian Bath*, 203.

Chapter V
Built and Unbuilt Visions

154 More than one hundred Adam drawings with bridges exist at Sir John Soane's Museum alone. The Scottish National Galleries also have a large collection. See: Ruddock, *Arch Bridges*, 116.

155 A. A. Tait, "The Picturesque Drawings of Robert Adam," *Master Drawings* 9, no. 2 (1971): 168.

156 Tait, *Robert Adam: Drawings and Imagination*, 162.

157 Tait, "The Picturesque Drawings of Robert Adam," 165. Tait dismisses the urge to attribute lower-quality drawings to James or William Adam, saying that while "it is tempting to attribute the weaker of Robert Adam's compositions to his brothers and assess them as shallow imitators ... Like any Artist, Adam had his off-day." See Tait, "The Picturesque Drawings of Robert Adam," 168.

158 Tait, *Robert Adam: Drawings and Imagination*, 156.

159 King, *The Complete Works*, 331.

160 Carolyn Susan Hales, *The Weathering of Sandstone on Historic Buildings: Culzean Castle, A Case Study. A Thesis Submitted to the Department of Geology & Applied Geology, University of Glasgow, in fulfilment of the degree of Doctor of Philosophy* (Glasgow: University of Glasgow, 1998).

161 Adam & Adam, *The Works*, 6.

162 Tait, *Robert Adam: Drawings and Imagination*, 118.

163 David King, *Unbuilt Adam* (Oxford: Architectural Press, 2001): 207. The evidence for the bridge's construction is spotty: the Soane Museum's catalogue cites its construction "with alterations," while the Historic England listing for Syon Park claims an Adam-designed bridge was built over one of "Capability" Brown's newly constructed lakes, but King includes the

work in his volume of unbuilt Adam designs. Further complicating matters is the fact that Adam lists the bridge as "over a branch of the river Thames" while the Charles Fowler bridge that purportedly replaced the Adam version crosses one of Brown's new lakes, a body of water not contiguous with the nearby Thames. See: SM Adam Volume 51/10[68]; "Syon Park," Historic England, https://historicengland.org.uk/listing/the-list/list-entry/1000148.

164 There exist two drawings of the bridge in the Soane Museum: SM Adam Volume 51/10(68) and 51/10(69). Ranald MacInnes sees the bridge as an elaborate architectural joke, but the presence of two plates for it in the *Works* and the detailed descriptions for the plates, in addition to the completely worked-up drawing at the Soane, suggest to me that it was designed for construction. See MacInnes, "Robert Adam's Bridges," 81–82.

165 This is further confirmed by his practical advice in the plate description: "if anyone shall copy this bridge, it must be placed neither in a deep valley, nor over a navigable river." See: Adam & Adam, *The Works in Architecture*, 8.

166 Adam & Adam, *The Works in Architecture*, 7.

167 Adam & Adam, *The Works in Architecture*, 8.

168 Adam & Adam, *The Works in Architecture*, 8.

169 Tait, *Robert Adam: Drawings and Imagination*, 110.

170 W. S. Lewis, *The Yale Edition of Horace Walpole's Correspondence*, Volume 38 (New Haven: Yale University Press, 1974): 428–29.

171 For more on their relationship, see John Wilton-Ely, "Style and Serendipity: Adam, Walpole and Strawberry Hill," *The British Art Journal* 11 (2011), No, 3, 3–14.

172 W. S. Lewis, *The Yale Edition of Horace Walpole's Correspondence*, Volume 32 (New Haven: Yale University Press, 1965): 125.

173 Lewis, *Walpole's Correspondence* Volume 28, 101–02.

174 Lewis, *Walpole's Correspondence* Volume 28, 108.

175 W. S. Lewis, *The Yale Edition of Horace Walpole's Correspondence*, Volume 33 (New Haven: Yale University Press, 1965): 498–500.

176 While Adam's plans for the South Bridge have received extensive attention and his sketches for the North Bridge are the subject of Alistair Rowan's article of 2004, his drawings for a bridge at the east end of Edinburgh's New Town, made in 1791, the year before

his death, have been mostly ignored. For a brief note on Adam's plans for the North Bridge, see Alistair Rowan, "Robert Adam's Ideas for the North Bridge in Edinburgh," *Architectural Heritage* XV (2004): 34–39. For an account of the South Bridge, including Adam's designs, see Andrew G. Fraser, *The Building of Old College: Adam, Playfair & the University of Edinburgh* (Edinburgh: Edinburgh University Press, 1989): 51–85. Ranald MacInnes discusses the Calton "bridge of communication" in two essays: "Robert Adam's Public Buildings," *Architectural Heritage* IV (1993): 13–19 and "Robert Adam's Bridges," 85.

177 Or, as Ranald MacInnes has it, the "Court Revival" style, given its similarity to Holyroodhouse. See MacInnes, "Robert Adam's Bridges," 15.

178 A. J. Youngson, *The Making of Classical Edinburgh: 1750–1840* (Edinburgh: Edinburgh University Press, 1962): 159. The castle style was allegedly endorsed by Adam to Craig in a passing comment.

179 Youngson, *The Making of Classical Edinburgh*, 135.

180 For a full discussion of Adam's return to Scotland, see Alistair Rowan, "After the Adelphi: Forgotten Years in the Adam Brothers' Practice," *Journal of the Royal Society of Arts* 122, no. 5218 (1974): 659–710.

181 The use of repeated blind arcades throughout the sketch of the Bridewell seen in the bridge drawing is the major clue that the building is a version of his classical prototype. Adam made several drawings and plans for the classical version, which was not built. These can be found in the Soane Museum's Adam volumes: 33/11, 20–25, 27; 2/50; 21/12.

182 SM Adam Volume 2/182 gives the most complete version of this design. SM Adam Volumes 4/130–31 and 54(VII)/255 give other, slightly altered versions in varying degrees of finish.

183 Ranald MacInnes, "Robert Adam's Public Buildings," 15.

184 In a funny coincidence, when the ravine was finally bridged in the 1810s, the Calton Bridge commissioners requested that it not be constructed "after the manner of Pulteney Bridge Bath," meaning without buildings on top, to secure the vista. Clearly Adam's triumphal design would not have suited. Minute Book, Calton Bridge Commissioners, 6 December 1815, quoted in Youngson, *The Making of Classical Edinburgh*, 142.

185 MacInnes, "Robert Adam's Public Buildings," 19.

Coda
Dalkeith Palace

186 Bolton, *The Architecture of Robert & James Adam*, Volume 1, 128.

187 Bolton, *The Architecture of Robert & James Adam*, Appendix, 9.

188 Colin McWilliam, *The Buildings of Scotland: Lothian Except Edinburgh* (New Haven and London: Yale University Press, 1978): 161. The third Duke's father died before succeeding.

189 E. P. Dennison & R. Coleman, *Historic Dalkeith: The Archaeological Implications of Development. The Scottish Burgh Survey Series* (Edinburgh: Centre for Scottish Urban History, 1988): 86.

190 Bolton, *The Architecture of Robert & James Adam*, Appendix, 9.

191 Dennison & Coleman, *Historic Dalkeith*, 85.

192 The acquisition number at the Yale Center for British Art is B1975.4.511.

193 McWilliam, *Lothian*, 158.

Bibliography

Adam, Keith. "Living with the Legend." *Architectural Heritage* IV (1993): 1–9

Adam, Robert and James Adam. *The Works in Architecture of Robert and James Adam, Esquires.* London: Printed for the Authors, 1778

Adam, William. *Vitruvius Scoticus: being a collection of plans, elevations, and sections of public buildings, noblemen's and gentlemen's houses in Scotland: principally from the designs of the late William Adams, Esq. architect.* Edinburgh: Printed for Adam Black, and J. & J. Robertson, 1810

Aymonino, Adriano. *Enlightened Eclecticism: the Grand Design of the 1st Duke and Duchess of Northumberland.* New Haven and London: Yale University Press, 2021

Aymonino, Adriano. "'The True Style of Antique Decoration': Agostino Brunias and the Birth of the Adam Style at Kedleston Hall and Syon House." In *Robert Adam and His Brothers: New Light on Britain's Leading Architectural Family*, edited by Colin Thom, 104–22. Swindon: Historic England, 2019

The Bath and Bristol Guide, or Tradesman's and Traveller's Pocket-Companion. Bath: Thomas Boddely, 1753

Bell, Amanda Lucy Victoria. "Robert Adam at Osterley and Syon: Giving 'a Modern Dress.'" Courtauld Institute of Art: unpublished MA dissertation, 2013

Bolton, Arthur T. *The Architecture and Decoration of Robert Adam and Sir John Soane, R.A. (1758–1837).* London: Wm. Clowes & Sons, 1920

Bolton, Arthur T. *The Architecture of Robert & James Adam (1758–1794).* London and New York: Scribner, 1922

Bonehill, John, and Stephen Daniels. *Paul Sandby: Picturing Britain.* London: Royal Academy of Arts, 2009

Bonehill, John. "'The Centre of Pleasure and Magnificence': Paul and Thomas Sandby's London." *Huntington Library Quarterly* 75, no. 3 (2012): 365–92

Borsay, Peter. *The English Urban Renaissance: Culture and Society in the Provincial Town, 1660–1770.* Oxford: Clarendon Press, 2002

Borsay, Peter. *The Image of Georgian Bath, 1700–2000: Towns, Heritage, and History.* Oxford: Oxford University Press, 2000

Briggs, Asa. *The Age of Improvement: A History of England.* London: Longmans, Green, 1959

Brink, Andrew. *Ink and Light: The Influence of Claude Lorrain's Etchings on England.* Montréal, Kingston, and London: McGill-Queen's University Press, for the Macdonald Stewart Art Centre, 2013

British Bridges: An Illustrated Technical and Historical Record. London: Organising Committee of the Public Works, Roads and Transport Congress, 1933

Brown, David Blayney, editor. *J. M. W. Turner: Sketchbooks, Drawings and Watercolours.* London: Tate Research Publication, November 2014

Brown, Ian Gordon. "Architects or Gentlemen? Adam Heraldry and its Implications." *Architectural Heritage* IV (1993): 82–92

Brown, Iain Gordon. "Robert Adam's Drawings: Edinburgh's Loss, London's Gain." *The Book of the Old Edinburgh Club,* New Series 2 (1992): 23–34

Brownell, Morris R. *Samuel Johnson's Attitude to the Arts.* Oxford: Clarendon Press, 1989

Buchan, James. *Crowded with Genius: The Scottish Enlightenment: Edinburgh's Moment of the Mind.* New York: HarperCollins, 2003

Butlin, R. A. and Robert A. Dodgshon. *An Historical Geography of England and Wales.* London: Academic Press, 1990

Cameron, Neil Manson. "Adam and 'Gothick' at Yester Chapel." *Architectural Heritage* IV (1993): 39–44

Chalklin, C. W. *English Counties and Public Building, 1650–1830.* London: Hambledon Press, 1998

Chalklin, C. W. *The Provincial Towns of Georgian England: A Study of the Building Process, 1740–1820.* Studies in Urban History 3. London: Edward Arnold, 1974

Christie, Manson & Woods. *Dumfries House: A Chippendale Commission*, Volumes I and II. London: Christie's, 2007

Crook, J. Mordaunt. "Northumbrian Gothick." *Journal of the Royal Society of Arts* 121, no. 5201 (1973): 271–83

Crook, J. Mordaunt. "The Pre-Victorian Architect: Professionalism & Patronage." *Architectural History* 12 (1969): 62–78

Clark, H. F. "Richard Payne Knight and the Picturesque Tradition." *The Town Planning Review* 19, no. 3/4 (1947): 144–52

Colvin, Howard. *A Biographical Dictionary of British Architects, 1600–1840, Third Edition.* New Haven and London: Yale University Press, 1995

Colvin, Howard. "The Beginnings of the Architectural Profession in Scotland." *Architectural History* 29 (1986): 168–82

Daniels, Stephen, with Susanne Seymour and Charles Watkins. "Landscaping and Estate Management in Later Georgian England." In *Garden History: Issues, Approaches, Methods,* edited by John Dixon Hunt, 359–371. Washington: Dumbarton Oaks Colloquium on the History of Landscape Architecture 13, 1992

De Maré, Eric Samuel. *The Bridges of Britain.* London: Batsford, 1954

Dennison, E. P. & R. Coleman, *Historic Dalkeith: The Archaeological Implications of Development. The Scottish Burgh Survey Series.* Edinburgh: Centre for Scottish Urban History, 1988

Desmarest, Clarisse Godard. "Introduction." In *The New Town of Edinburgh: An Architectural Celebration,* edited by Clarisse Godard Desmarest, 1–18. Edinburgh: John Donald, 2019

Drury, P. and Ian Gow. *Audley End, Essex*. London: English Heritage, 1984

Drury, P. *Audley End*. London: English Heritage, 2004

Finch, Jonathan and Katherine Giles. *Estate Landscapes: Design, Improvement and Power in the Post-Medieval Landscape: Papers given at the Estate Landscapes Conference, April 2003, Hosted by the Society for Post-Medieval Archaeology*. Society for Post-Medieval Archaeology Monographs 4. Woodbridge: Boydell & Brewer, 2007

Fleming, John. *Robert Adam and His Circle: In Edinburgh & Rome*. London: John Murray, 1962

Fraser, Andrew G. and Ian Gow. "An Academic Pursuit." *Architectural Heritage* IV (1993): 101–106

Fraser, Andrew G. *The Building of Old College: Adam, Playfair & the University of Edinburgh*. Edinburgh: Edinburgh University Press, 1989

Gifford, John and Colin McWilliam, David Walker and Christopher Wilson. *The Buildings of Scotland: Edinburgh*. New Haven and London: Yale University Press, 2003

Gifford, John. *William Adam, 1689–1748: The Life and Times of Scotland's Universal Architect*. Edinburgh: Mainstream Publishing, 1989

Gifford, John. "William Adam and the Historians." *Architectural Heritage* I (1990): 1–7

Girouard, Mark. *A Country House Companion*. New Haven and London: Yale University Press, 1987

Girouard, Mark. *Life in the English Country House*. New Haven and London: Yale University Press, 1978

Girouard, Mark. *The English Town*. New Haven and London: Yale University Press, 1990

Goodsir, Sally. "George Steuart and Robert Adam: A Professional Relationship Revealed," *The Georgian Group Journal* XVIII (2010): 91–104

Gow, Ian. "William Adam: A Planner of Genius." *Architectural Heritage* I (1990): 62–73

Green, Simon. *Dumfries House: An Architectural Story*. Edinburgh: Royal Commission on the Ancient and Historical Monuments of Scotland, 2014

Hales, Carolyn Susan. *The Weathering of Sandstone on Historic Buildings: Culzean Castle, A Case Study. A Thesis Submitted to the Department of Geology & Applied Geology, University of Glasgow, in fulfilment of the degree of Doctor of Philosophy*. Glasgow: University of Glasgow, 1998

Harris, Bob. "Towns, Improvement and Cultural Change in Georgian Scotland: The Evidence of the Angus Burghs c. 1760–1820." *Urban History* 33, 2 (2006): 195–212

Harris, Eileen. *Osterley Park, Middlesex*. London: National Trust, 1994

Harris, Eileen. *The Genius of Robert Adam: His Interiors*. New Haven and London: Yale University Press for the Paul Mellon Centre for Studies in British Art, 2001

Harris, John and Michael Snodin. *Sir William Chambers: Architect to George III*. New Haven and London: Yale University Press, 1996

Harris, Leslie and Gervase Jackson-Stops. *Robert Adam and Kedleston: The Making of a Neo-Classical Masterpiece*. London: National Trust, 1987

Harris, Stuart. "New Light on the First New Town." *The Book of the Old Edinburgh Club*, New Series 2 (1992):1–14

Hausberg, Miranda. "Robert Adam's Scenographic Interiors." In *Robert Adam and His Brothers: New Light on Britain's Leading Architectural Family*, edited by Colin Thom, 123–141. Swindon: Historic England, 2019

Hawksmoor, Nicholas. *A Short Historical Account of London-Bridge, With a Proposition for a New Stone-Bridge at Westminster: As Also an Account of Some Remarkable Stone-Bridges Abroad, and What the Best Authors Have Said and Directed Concerning The Methods of Building Them*. London: J. Wilcox, 1736

"Heston and Isleworth: Syon House," in *A History of the County of Middlesex: Volume 3, Shepperton, Staines, Stanwell, Sunbury, Teddington, Heston and Isleworth, Twickenham, Cowley, Cranford, West Drayton, Greenford, Hanwell, Harefield and Harlington*, edited by Susan Reynolds, 97–100. London: Victoria County History, 1962

Holmes, Oliver Wendell. *The Autocrat of the Breakfast-Table: Every Man His Own Boswell*. Boston: Houghton, Mifflin and Company, 1895

Hoyle, R. W., editor. *Custom, Improvement and the Landscape in Early Modern Britain*. Farnham: Ashgate, 2011

Ison, Walter. *The Georgian Buildings of Bath: From 1700 to 1830*. Revised edition. Bath: Kingsmead, 1980

Johnson, Samuel. *The Letters of Samuel Johnson*. Volume I: 1719–1774. Collected & Edited by R. W. Chapman. Oxford: Clarendon Press, 1952

Kay, William. "Robert Adam: Some Responses to a Scottish Background." *Architectural Heritage* IV (1993): 23–38

Kay, William R. M. "What's His Line: Would the Real William Adam Please Stand Up? Some Recent Research Discoveries." *Architectural Heritage* I (1990): 49–61

"Kenwood." In *Survey of London: Volume 17, The Parish of St Pancras Part 1: The Village of Highgate*, edited by Percy Lovell and William Marcham, 114–32. London: London County Council, 1936

King, David. "In Search of Adam." *Architectural Heritage* IV (1993): 93–100

King, David. *The Complete Works of Robert and James Adam*. Oxford: Architectural Press, 2001

King, David. "The Ingenious Mr Adam." In *Robert Adam and His Brothers: New Light on Britain's Leading Architectural Family*, edited by Colin Thom, 183–201. Swindon: Historic England, 2019

King, David. *Unbuilt Adam*. Oxford: Architectural Press, 2001

Knox, James. *The Scottish Country House*. New York: Vendome Press, 2012

Lewis, Murray "Georgian New Towns of Glasgow and Edinburgh." In *The New Town of Edinburgh: An Architectural Celebration*, edited by Clarisse Godard Desmarest, 78–96. Edinburgh: John Donald, 2019

Lewis, W. S. *The Yale Edition of Horace Walpole's Correspondence*, Volume 28. New Haven: Yale University Press, 1955

Lewis, W. S. *The Yale Edition of Horace Walpole's Correspondence*, Volume 32. New Haven: Yale University Press, 1965

Lewis, W. S. *The Yale Edition of Horace Walpole's Correspondence*, Volume 33. New Haven: Yale University Press, 1965

Lewis, W. S. *The Yale Edition of Horace Walpole's Correspondence*, Volume 38. New Haven: Yale University Press, 1974

Lindfield, Peter N. "A 'Classical Goth': Robert Adam's Engagement with Medieval Architecture." In *Robert Adam and His Brothers: New Light on Britain's Leading Architectural Family*, edited by Colin Thom, 161–82. Swindon: Historic England, 2019

Lindsay, Ian G. and Mary Cosh. *Inveraray and the Dukes of Argyll*. Edinburgh: Edinburgh University Press, 1973

MacInnes, Ranald. "Edinburgh Old Town and New Town: A Tale of One City?" In *The New Town of Edinburgh: An Architectural Celebration*, edited by Clarisse Godard Desmarest, 234–50. Edinburgh: John Donald, 2019

MacInnes, Ranald. "'My Mother's Dear British Boy." In *Living with Jacobitism: The Three Kingdoms and Beyond*, edited by Allan I. Macinnes, Kieran German, and Lesley Graham, 173–84. London: Pickering & Chatto, 2014

MacInnes, Ranald. "Robert Adam's Bridges." In *The Architecture of Scottish Cities: Essays in Honour of David Walker*, edited by Deborah Mays, 78–86. East Linton: Tuckwell Press, 1997

MacInnes, Ranald. "Robert Adam's Public Buildings." *Architectural Heritage* IV (1993): 10–22

MacInnes, Ranald. "'Rubblemania': Ethic and Aesthetic in Scottish Architecture." *Journal of Design History* 9 (1996): 137–51

MacInnes, Ranald. "Was Scotland a 'Narrow Place?'" In *The Architecture of Scotland*, edited by Louisa Humm, John Lowrey, and Aonghus MacKechnie. Edinburgh: Edinburgh University Press, 2020

MacKechnie, Aonghus "Scotland's Planned Towns and Villages Over the Centuries." In *The New Town of Edinburgh: An Architectural Celebration*, edited by Clarisse Godard Desmarest, 41–63. Edinburgh: John Donald, 2019

Manco, Jean. "Pulteney Bridge." *Architectural History* 38 (1995): 129–45

Mayer, Laura. "Landscape as Legacy: Elizabeth Percy, 1st Duchess of Northumberland, and the Gothick Garden Buildings of Alnwick, Northumberland." *Garden History* 39, no.1 (2011): 34–50

McFetrich, David. *An Encylopaedia of British Bridges*. Yorkshire: Pen and Sword Transport, 2019

McKee, Kirsten Carter. *Calton Hill: And the Plans for Edinburgh's Third New Town*. Edinburgh: John Donald, 2018

McWilliam, Colin. *The Buildings of Scotland: Lothian Except Edinburgh*. New Haven and London: Yale University Press, 1978

Mowl, Tim. *Palladian Bridges: Prior Park and the Whig Connection*. Bath: Millstream Books in association with the Bath Preservation Trust, 1993

Musson, Jeremy. *Robert Adam: Country House Design, Decoration & the Art of Elegance*. New York: Rizzoli, 2017

Neale, R. S. *Bath 1680–1850: A Social History or A Valley of Pleasure, Yet a Sink of Iniquity*. London: Routledge & Kegan Paul, 1981

Nenadic, Stana. "Architect-Builders in London and Edinburgh, c. 1750–1800, and the Market for Expertise." *The Historical Journal* 55, 3 (2012): 597–617

Oppé, Paul. "Robert Adam's Picturesque Compositions." *The Burlington Magazine for Connoisseurs* 80, no. 468 (1942): 54, 56–57, 59

Pawson, Eric. *Transport and Economy: The Turnpike Roads of Eighteenth Century Britain.* London and New York: Academic Press, 1977

Pevsner, Nikolaus and James Bettley. *Essex.* Pevsner Architectural Guides. New Haven and London: Yale University Press, 2007

Pittock, Murray "Edinburgh: Smart City of 1700." In *The New Town of Edinburgh: An Architectural Celebration*, edited by Clarisse Godard Desmarest, 19–40. Edinburgh: John Donald, 2019

Publicus [Robert Mylne]. *Observations on Bridge Building, and the Several Plans Offered for a New Bridge.* London: J. Townsend, 1760

Richardson, A. E. *Robert Mylne, Architect and Engineer: 1733 to 1811.* London: Batsford, 1955

Robert Adam at Home, 1728–1978: Drawings from the collection of Blair Adam. Edinburgh: West Register House, 1978

Robertson, Iain A. "The Earl of Kinnoull's Bridge: The Construction of the Bridge of Tay at Perth, 1763–1772." *Journal of Scottish Historical Studies* 6 (1986): 18–32

Robinson, John Martin. *Georgian Model Farms: A Study of Decorative and Model Farm Buildings in the Age of Improvement, 1700–1846.* Oxford: Clarendon Press, 1983

Rowan, Alistair. "After the Adelphi: Forgotten Years in the Adam Brothers' Practice." *Journal of the Royal Society of Arts* 122, no. 5218 (1974): 659–710

Rowan, Alistair. *"Bob the Roman": Heroic Antiquity & the Architecture of Robert Adam.* London: Sir John Soane's Museum, 2003

Rowan, Alistair. "Johnnie, the Eldest Adam Brother." In *Robert Adam and His Brothers: New Light on Britain's Leading Architectural Family*, edited by Colin Thom, 36–62. Swindon: Historic England, 2019

Rowan, Alistair. "Kinross and Edinburgh: Some Ideas of Robert Adam on the Proper Improvement of Towns." In *The Architecture of Scottish Cities: Essays in Honour of David Walker*, edited by Deborah Mays, 70–77. East Linton: Tuckwell Press, 1997

Rowan, Alistair. "Robert Adam's Ideas for the North Bridge in Edinburgh." *Architectural Heritage* XV (2004): 34–39

Rowan, Alistair. *Vaulting Ambition: The Adam Brothers: Contractors to the Metropolis in the Reign of George III.* London: Sir John Soane's Museum, 2007

Rowan, Alistair. "William Adam's Library." *Architectural Heritage* I (1990): 8–33

Ruddock, Ted. *Arch Bridges and Their Builders, 1735–1835.* Cambridge: Cambridge University Press, 1979

Saint, Andrew. *Architect and Engineer: A Study in Sibling Rivalry.* New Haven and London: Yale University Press, 2007

Sanderson, Margaret H. B. "Robert Adam's Last Visit to Scotland, 1791." *Architectural History* 25 (1982): 35–46

Sanderson, Margaret H. B. "Trivial Pursuit? Portrait of the Artist in Letters and Diaries." *Architectural Heritage* IV (1993): 66–81

Sands, Frances. *Robert Adam's London.* Oxford: Archaeopress, 2016

Shrimpton, Colin. *Alnwick Castle: Home of the Duke of Northumberland.* Derby: Heritage House Group, 2004

Simpson & Brown, for the Great Steward of Scotland's Dumfries House Trust. *Draft Conservation Plan: Introduction & Historical Development*, Volume 1. Edinburgh: Simpson & Brown, 2008

Skempton, A. W and P. S. M. Cross-Rudkin. *A Biographical Dictionary of Civil Engineers in Great Britain and Ireland.* London: Thomas Telford, 2002

Sonnabend, Martin, and Jon Whitely, with Christian Rümelin. *Claude Lorrain: The Enchanted Landscape.* Oxford: Ashmolean Museum in Association with Lund Humphries, 2011

Smeaton, John. *Mr. Smeaton's Answer to the Misrepresentations of His Plan for Black-Friars Bridge, Contained in a Late Anonymous Pamphlet, Addressed to the Gentlemen of the Committee for Building a Bridge at Black-Friars.* London: 1760

Spooner, Sarah. *Regions and Designed Landscapes in Georgian England.* Abingdon: Routledge, 2016

Stewart, Margaret. "City and State in the Designs of the 6th Earl of Mar." In *The New Town of Edinburgh: An Architectural Celebration*, edited by Clarisse Godard Desmarest, 64–77. Edinburgh: John Donald, 2019

Stewart, Margaret. *The Architectural Landscape and Constitutional Plans of the Earl of Mar, 1700–32.* Dublin: Four Courts Press, 2016

Stillman, Damie. *English Neo-Classical Architecture.* London: Zwemmer, 1988

Summerson, John. *Georgian London*, edited by Howard Colvin. New Haven: Published for the Paul Mellon Centre for Studies in British Art by Yale University Press, 2003

"Syon Park." Historic England. https://historicengland.org.uk/listing/the-list/list-entry/1000148

Tait, A. A. "Reading the Ruins: Robert Adam and Piranesi in Rome." *Architectural History* 27 (1984): 524–33

Tait, A. A. "Robert Adam's Picturesque Architecture." *The Burlington Magazine* 123, no. 940 (1981): 421–24

Tait, A. A. *Robert Adam: Drawings and Imagination.* Cambridge Studies in the History of Architecture. Cambridge: Cambridge University Press, 1993

Tait, A. A. *Robert Adam: The Creative Mind: From the Sketch to the Finished Drawing.* London: Sir John Soane's Museum, 1996

Tait, A. A. "The Picturesque Drawings of Robert Adam." *Master Drawings* 9, no. 2 (1971): 161–220

Tarlow, Sarah. *The Archaeology of Improvement in Britain, 1750–1850.* Cambridge Studies in Archaeology. Cambridge and New York: Cambridge University Press, 2007

Thom, Colin. "Introduction. 'Some Promising Young Men': Robert Adam and His Brothers." In *Robert Adam and His Brothers: New light on Britain's Leading Architectural Family*, edited by Colin Thom, 1–35. Swindon: Historic England, 2019

Trotter, Marrikka. "Temporal Sublime: Robert Adam's Castle Style and Geology in the Scottish Enlightenment". In *Robert Adam and His Brothers: New Light on Britain's Leading Architectural Family*, edited by Colin Thom, 223–38. Swindon: Historic England, 2019

Ward, Robert. *The Man Who Buried Nelson: The Surprising Life of Robert Mylne*. London: Tempus, 2007

Watkin, David, editor. *Sale Catalogues of Libraries of Eminent Persons: Volume 4: Architects*. London: Mansell with Sotheby Parke-Bernet Publications, 1972

Watkin, David, editor. *Sir John Soane: Enlightenment Thought and the Royal Academy Lectures*. Cambridge: Cambridge University Press, 1996

Williams, J. D. "The Landowner as Manager." *Essex Journal* 15 (1980): 74–82

Williams, J. D. *Audley End: The Restoration of 1762–1797*. Essex Record Office. Chelmsford: Essex County Council (Record Office), 1966

Williamson, Tom. *Polite Landscapes: Garden and Society in Eighteenth-century England*. Stroud, Gloucestershire: Allan Sutton, 1995

Williamson, Tom. *The Transformation of Rural England: Farming and the Landscape 1700–1870*. Exeter: University of Exeter Press, 2002

Wilton-Ely, John. "'Gingerbread and Sippets of Embroidery': Horace Walpole and Robert Adam." *Eighteenth-Century Life* 25, no. 2 (2001): 147–69

Wilton-Ely, John. "Style and Serendipity: Adam, Walpole and Strawberry Hill." *The British Art Journal* 11, no. 3 (2011): 3–14

Wood, John. *A Description of Bath*. London: W. Bathoe and T. Lownds, 1765

Woodley, Roger. "A Very Mortifying Situation': Robert Mylne's Struggle to Get Paid for Blackfriars Bridge." *Architectural History* 43 (2000): 172–86

Worsley, Giles. "Alnwick Castle, Northumberland II: The 18th-Century Restoration." *Country Life* (December 8, 1988): 74–78

Wylson, Anthony. *Aquatecture: Architecture and Water*. London: The Architectural Press, 1986

Youngson, A. J. *The Making of Classical Edinburgh: 1750–1840*. Edinburgh: Edinburgh University Press, 1966

Index

Acknowledgments

It's tempting, in thanking those who have helped to make this book possible, to engage in an extended metaphor about bridge components. Someone could be the spandrels, someone else the voussoirs, until at last the book stands like a masonry bridge. But I am not clever enough to make the metaphor work, and so these appreciations will have to be conventional. First thanks must go to Clive Aslet and Dylan Thomas, not just the publishers of this book but dear friends. I can still remember, sodden though the night was, when Dylan first asked when Triglyph would get to publish my book. At that point a book idea didn't even exist, but now idea is reality, and it is thanks to Clive and Dylan that it is so. Dylan also receives special commendation for the beautiful photographs that illustrate this book, bringing to life Adam's bridges in a way my words are not equipped to do. Extra points are due to Dylan for navigating the red Vauxhall hither and yon across Britain, through conditions that might be described as "challenging." Kate Turner ensured that "the boys" never got lost on the road and that the production of this book never got lost either. Its appearance, on time, is down to her. Ines Cross offered helpful suggestions on the manuscript and displayed great marketing prowess.

Paul Tilby is responsible for the design, Sheila Hill the index, and Mike Turner the proofreading. They all have my thanks.

On our own "fanciful and picturesque" tour, Dylan and I were graciously welcomed at every turn. The Buccleuch Living Heritage Trust arranged access to Dalkeith Palace, our first stop and a harbinger of all the good light that followed. At Alnwick Castle, the Duke and Duchess of Northumberland granted us free rein over various fields, ensuring that every angle of the Lion Bridge could be surveyed. The cover of the book is the happy result. The Prince's Foundation welcomed us on site at Dumfries House with properly *dreich* Scottish weather, while the staff at the Lodge was ready with a well-timed dram. The after-hours access to Culzean Castle offered to us by the National Trust for Scotland ensured that our final stop up north was a great success; you never know when the sun will come out.

Roger Kimball has been my champion for years. He leads *The New Criterion* without fear, and if a modicum of that fearlessness has been instilled in me then I am fortunate. A model for us all, Roger also supported this project from the start, offering logistical wherewithal, advice, and encouragement throughout. The rest of the staff at *The New Criterion* has my thanks for creating a work environment that invigorates serious inquiry but which never takes itself too seriously.

Sam Schneider, Lauren Miklos, and Rebecca Hecht kept me sane enough to finish the manuscript.

Dominic Green has offered much guidance from this project's earliest days, and his publication of my travel diary in *The Spectator* convinced me that someone else might actually want to read this book.

My interest in Robert Adam dates back to my undergraduate days, when I had the good fortune to study for a term at the University of Edinburgh. Dartmouth College, and the Frank family, later funded travel relating to my senior thesis on Adam's Charlotte Square, which set me on this path. Coincidentally, my Edinburgh digs were on Chambers Street, site of the long-demolished Adam Square, which had been built by the Adams and was knocked down for the building of the South Bridge. Robert Adam had submitted proposals for that bridge that were rejected for cost; one sympathizes. Meanwhile, my Edinburgh family—Gary, Denise, Antonia, Fergus, and Liam Kildare—has been there every step of the way, offering hospitality and above all fun on multiple continents.

This book builds substantially off of coursework done at the Courtauld Institute of Art, where I was blessed to study under Christine Stevenson, who taught me how to mine quarries in architectural history. My classmate there, Harry Adams, has kept me abreast of developments in the scholarly world while also being a boon companion for Nairn walks in London.

Carolyn and the late and daily missed James Penrose graciously lent me their flat while I was back in London conducting research, but such generosity is mere sea spray compared to the oceans of support and warmth they have shown over the years in London, Paris, and Cragsmoor. David and Clarissa Pryce-Jones have been similarly beneficent, never failing to have me for dinner, whether in London or Florence, and no matter the weather.

Professor Jeremy Black offered specialist advice on the nature of Robert Adam's grand tour, and who better to ask?

The Soane Museum, that magnificent repository of the bulk of Robert Adam's surviving drawings, provided for the reproduction of many of them here, and Nathan Emery facilitated this with great efficiency. The Yale Center for British Art was also munificent with reproductions.

Peter Pennoyer and Gregory Gilmartin explained to me how architectural publishing was meant to work and were endlessly patient with my questions. Their model guides the way.

Corrie Stuttaford has been a constant source of wisdom, and her keen eye for the main chance has proved essential. Andrew Stuttaford's good sense and Harold Stuttaford's good cheer have buoyed me.

Simon Heffer adorned this book with a sparkling foreword, for which he has my everlasting thanks.

Above all stand my parents, who have been the piers on this bridge (I couldn't resist), rooting it to the ground and making sure it remains standing. Their undying love and support is miraculous, and they have my eternal gratitude.

Illustration credits

With thanks to:

Dalkeith Country Park: p118, 122–123, 125, 149, back cover

Duke and Duchess of Northumberland: front cover, p58, 60–61, 64–67, 70–71, 130, 137

National Trust for Scotland: p7, 96–105, 146

The Prince's Foundation: p8, 18, 20–30, 126

First published in the United Kingdom in 2023 by Triglyph Books.

Triglyph Books
154 Tachbrook Street
London SW1V 2NE

www.triglyphbooks.com
Instagram: @triglyphbooks

Designed by Paul Tilby
www.paultilby.com

Publisher: Clive Aslet and Dylan Thomas
Production Manager: Kate Turner
Assistant Editor: Ines Cross
Production Coordinator: Claire Mercer
Proofreader: Mike Turner

British Library Cataloguing-in-Publication Data.
A catalogue record for this book is available from the British Library.

ISBN : 978-1-9163554-7-7

Printed and bound sustainably in Italy.